I0828601

In tali nunquam lassat venatio sylva.
A.D.1884.

TO THE MEMORY

OF THE

Architect and of the Members of the Building Committee

OF THE

CROWN INN,

WHOSE LABORS PROVOKED THIS HISTORICAL EXCURSION,

AND TO MY FRIEND,

JOHN W. JORDAN,

OF PHILADELPHIA,

Late Commissary Sergeant of "Starr's Battery," 32d Regiment P. M.,

I DEDICATE ITS PAGES.

"NOW this Indenture witnesseth: That for and in consideration of the sum of two hundred pounds, lawful money of Pennsylvania, unto the said John Simpson, by the hands of his said attorney, William Allen, well and truly paid at and before the sealing and delivery hereof, he, the said John Simpson, hath granted, bargained, sold, released, and confirmed, and by his said attorney, William Allen, doth hereby grant, bargain, sell, release, and confirm unto Jasper Payne, of Bethlehem, in the county of Bucks, in the Province of Pennsylvania, wine-cooper, and to his heirs and assigns, all that the said piece or tract of land, containing as aforesaid, two hundred and seventy-four acres, together, also, with all and singular the buildings, improvements, ways, roads, waters, water-courses, rights, liberties, privileges, hereditaments, and appurtenances whatsoever thereto belonging, or in any wise appertaining, and the reversions and remainders thereof."

JOHN SIMPSON,

BY HIS ATTORNEY,

WILLIAM ALLEN, Esq.,

TO

JASPER PAYNE,

For 274 Acres.

Philadelphia, 3 *June*, 1746.

UNTIL some painstaking antiquary shall have fully illumined the twilight, by which, it must be confessed, the history of the old Crown Inn (despite the acumen of diverse recent interpreters) is, even yet, imperfectly read,—the following pages are offered to the interested reader, in the hope that they may partially supply a want. Meanwhile, let him abide the time until the end, so devoutly wished for by him, shall be satisfactorily attained.

It may be well to observe that what is here written, occasionally militates against what the writer and others have written on this subject—a confession, however, which cannot shake the intelligent reader's confidence in either—he well knowing that historical narrative, like all other kinds of writing, is liable to err, and is at best but an approximation to the truth.

For the rest, the following pages are based upon authentic records. If they aid in recalling the past, and prove potent in peopling its realm with the memories of departed heroes, the object in writing them will be amply fulfilled.

BETHLEHEM, PENNA., *September* 1, 1872.

The Crown Inn near Bethlehem.

1745.

BLIND, indeed, to the perfections of God's handiwork in Nature, and inlets to a sluggish soul, must be the eyes that fail to see, or that grow weary of resting upon the beauties of the landscape which skirts the border of the bluff, on whose ridge, in sharp relief against the northern sky, stands the modern borough of Bethlehem.

From the placid stream which comes to view out of the recesses of a fairy island, as from some hiding place, the foldings of gentle hills rise upward and higher, until their swelling outlines blend with the mountain which locks in its embrace this perfect little world. Whatever of beauty in form, whether form of headland, lowland or upland,—whatever of beauty in grouping, be it that of foliage, with sky or cloud, or heaven-reflecting water,—whatever of grateful charm in the alternation of forest with ploughed or seeded field, of green nook with fallow wold, of gray with sombre hues,—follow the sweep of the sunny amphitheatre before you, and say—are not all these here? No other portion of the valley of the Lehigh, confessedly, has been favored by Nature as this; none, elsewhere, perhaps, of the same extent, as much; and yet even here, this goddess, strange to say, has planted a garden within a garden, which man is now adorning with all that is chaste in rural art or magnificent in suburban architecture. Would you mete out the bounds of this garden-spot,—taking the river for a base, run a line from a point in its right bank not a stone's throw below the upper bridge due south, run a second parallel to this, from its bank where the stream bends gracefully around Calypso Island, through the laurels and rockeries of Oppelt's and the embowered precincts of Bishopthorpe, and complete the rude parallelogram with the southern horizon by way of head-line. This is the frame in which is set "the Picture in the Valley." View it from what point you choose, (best, perhaps, from the iron bridge that spans the Menagassi),—it is ever a picture of surpassing loveliness. A painting not made by human hand, it defies criticism; a painting made by a master, it requires no tedious study,—so just are its proportions, so truthful its perspective, so correct its distances and foreshortening, so harmonious the blending of its colors and its contrasts of light and shade, so real the transparency of its atmosphere, and so perfectly natural its stereoscopic effects. View it when you may, it never fails to please. With the change of the season or the hour of the day, its aspect, indeed, varies, but only to reveal new shapes and tints, with which to challenge the beholder's silent admiration. It is all bathed in sunlight, long before you see the spokes of the shining chariot in the east, and long after the lower world is wrapt in the mists that gather nightly over the river. Well may you ask, is it a city of gold, half-hidden among trees of gold, that looms up on those aerial heights, growing hourly more luminous, until under the meridian sun, it burns and dazzles in a glory of consuming splendor? But would you view it in its loveliest mood, (be it the time of tender buds or of green leaves, or when maples flame on every side,)—mark the witchery that steals over the scene, as soon as the noonday's glare begins to wane and the evening hours come on. How gentle the spirit that then breathes on hill and tree and turret, blending their shapes and softening their hues and mellowing their lights! How silently the shadows creep down the grassy slopes, stretching out their toils farther and farther across the lowland, until, when the sun has sunk behind the hills of Oppelt's, they hold all things spell-bound in neutral tints and deepening shade,—there being naught to indicate that the landscape is not dead, but merely asleep in trance,—save the rosy blush athwart the mountain top and the glittering fanions on the great tower of Packer Hall! Then lies before you, the picture in the valley, in its loveliest mood!

It was within the precincts of this garden-spot, that, more than one hundred and twenty-five years ago, there lay what was called by the Moravians of that time "the Simpson Tract," on which was reared for the refreshing of all who had occasion to wayfare through a then almost primitive wilderness, the humble hostelry whose name is borne on the title page of this tribute to its memory.

Now, the naked deed-history of this, to the reader, important tract of land, is the following:

By indentures of lease and release bearing dates of 22d and 23d of October, 1681, respectively, William Penn, Sr., Proprietary and Chief Governor of the Province of Pennsylvania, by the name of William Penn, of Worminghurst, in the County of Sussex, Esq., bargained, sold and confirmed to William Lowther and Margaret Lowther, two of the children of Anthony Lowther, Esq., by Margaret, his wife,* five thousand

* Margaret Lowther, was a sister of William Penn (2 Proud, p. 115). She married Anthony Lowther, of Masham, in the wapentake of Hang-East, North Riding, of the County of York. Their children were William and Margaret Lowther. William Lowther married Catharine Preston; their child was Thomas Lowther. Margaret Lowther married Benjamin Poole; their child was Mary Poole. Mary Poole married Richard Nichols; and their child was Margaret Nichols.

acres of land in the Province of Pennsylvania, to be set out in such places or parts of said Province, and at such times as were agreed upon between said parties,—for a certain specified consideration, and on the payment of the chief or quitrent of one shilling for every hundred acres, on the first day of March, forever, in lieu of all services and demands whatsoever.

Margaret Lowther, who, on the decease of her brother William, had been invested with his moiety of the original grant, devised the entire tract to her daughter, Margaret Poole.

Margaret Poole, soon after marrying John Nichols, of Coney Hutch, in the County of Middlesex, Esq., jointly with her husband conveyed the aforesaid proportion and quantity of five thousand acres, by indenture bearing date of 23d of September, 1731, to Joseph Stanwix, of Bartlett's Buildings, Holborn, gentleman.

Joseph Stanwix released them to John Simpson, of Tower Hill, London, merchant, in January of 1732; whereupon the latter, desirous of transmuting his colonial estates into pounds, shillings and pence sterling, caused, by virtue of a Proprietary's warrant, bearing date of 31st October, 1733, a parcel of two hundred and seventy-four acres and allowance of the noble grant, to be located and surveyed for his own use,—and subsequently others.* Now the parcel with

* A second parcel of the Lowther Tract, to wit, 200 acres adjoining the Barony of Nazareth, due south of Christian's Spring, was surveyed for

which this writing is concerned, the one last stated as containing two hundred and seventy-four acres, was located on the West Branch of Delaware,* in Lower Saucon township, in the County of Bucks, the survey being made on the 24th of November, 1736, by Nicholas Scull,† at that time a deputy for William Parsons, Surveyor General. Thereupon it was thrown into the market.

The Moravian Brethren, on establishing themselves within the Forks of Delaware (the first house of

---

Simpson, by Scull, on the 26th of October, 1736, and deeded by Allen to John Okely, of Bethlehem, for the use of the Moravians, on the 19th of July, 1751.

* The name by which the Lehigh river is always designated in early deeds and surveys.

† Nicholas Scull, who played a prominent part in the early annals of Pennsylvania, is first met with at White Marsh, where he was residing, in 1722, engaged as a surveyor, and occasionally in the public service, acting in Indian affairs in the capacity of a runner, or as interpreter for the Delawares. With Godfrey, Parsons, and other young men of inquiring minds, Scull was associated in Franklin's Junta Club, and there "manifested a fondness for making verses." In 1744 he was appointed Sheriff of the city and County of Philadelphia, and in June of 1748, succeeded William Parsons as Surveyor General. This position he filled till in December of 1761. Meanwhile, he had drawn a map of the improved part of the Province, which was published by an Act of Parliament in January of 1759. Scull was Sheriff of Northampton for three terms (1753 to 1755), and in those years was a resident of Easton. In 1757 we find him in Philadelphia, and in 1764, keeping an inn at Reading. His sons, James, Peter, William, Edward and Jasper were all surveyors. William published a map of the Province in 1770. Both father and sons were associated with the Moravians, by business, for a number of years.

Bethlehem was blocked up in the spring of 1741), soon perceived that special advantages would accrue to them from the possession of the "Simpson Tract," opposite their settlement. "It will give us the control of the river at this point, and an unobstructed outlet into the more thickly peopled parts of the Province. Once in other hands," they argued, "and we may be perpetually embarrassed." Reasoning thus, they lost no time, too, in arranging the preliminaries for an early purchase. But these, much to their regret, involved a case of ejectment, in as far as Conrad Ruetschi, a fellow countryman of Orgetorix and William Tell, who had been imported in the ship Mercury, of London, William Wilson, master, but last from Cowes, in May of 1735,—was firmly seated on the premises in the memorable spring of 1741. The ring of the Moravians' axes, and the crash of falling trees on the hillside north of the river, in the stormy March of that year, sounded like a knell of doom in the ears of the Helvetian squatter. He admitted that he had been headed off, and that he was likely to be outflanked, too; yet, feeling strong in the nine points of the law, he abated none in improving the surroundings of his cabin, turning his attention also to the growing of flax. The first crop of this staple that matured on the Simpson Tract, it may interest some reader to know, was gathered for Ruetschi, by the hired labor of the

Moravian women of Bethlehem. This was on the 27th of July, 1742, falling, therefore, in times of Dorian simplicity, but a little in advance of those in which our common mother span. So trifling an occurrence would not have been adduced in this narrative, but for the inference it enables us to draw, to wit, that the Moravians and their Swiss neighbor were still living side by side in apparently perfect harmony. But when in Februray of 1743, the former were hopefully negotiating with William Allen,* of Philadelphia,

* William Allen, whose speculative enterprise opened up the Forks of Delaware (subsequent to 1752, Northampton County) to settlement, and whose name is perpetuated on hundreds of deeds executed by him on the sale of their lands to early purchasers, was, we are told by Proud (2 p. 188), "the son of William Allen, Sr., an eminent merchant of Philadelphia, a considerable promoter of the trade of the Province, and a man of good character and estate." The subject of this memoir, it is asserted by Charles Thomson, deeded away lands in the Minisinks (near Stroudsburgh) as early as 1733, four years prior, therefore, to the confirmation of the old Indian purchase, or the extinction of the Indian claim, by the historic day and a half day's walk. Being "on the ground floor," (to use a lofty figure of speech) accordingly, and shrewd and prudent, forsooth, he was successful in operating and acquired a handsome fortune. This gave him,—naturally enough, position,—and state following on its heels, Mr. Allen, in 1761 (see 1 Watson, p. 208), was one of but three gentlemen in the capital of the Province who rode in carriages of their own, his equipage being a Landau drawn by four blacks, and driven by an expert of a whip, specially imported from England. But fortune extended his influence also, and being respected for probity and a knowledge of the law, he, in due course of time, was appointed Chief Justice of the Province (1750), sitting as such on the woolsack down to the time of the rupture between the colonies and the mother country (1774), when with

merchant, the duly appointed attorney-at-law of John Simpson, of Tower Hill, London, for the purchase of the two hundred and seventy-four acres and allowance, and when on the 11th day of March ensuing, the latter saw the great flat for the Bethlehem ferry launched and propelled under the very walls of his stronghold, aggrieved beyond endurance, he broke truce. Turning to the law for redress, he appealed to Nathaniel Irish,* the nearest Justice of the Peace,

other loyalists whose fortunes were linked with those of the old regime, he sailed for England. He died in London in 1780. His wife, who was a daughter of Andrew Hamilton, an eminent lawyer, bore him three sons, Andrew, William, and James. The first was Chief Justice a short time in the commencement of the Revolution, and also a member of Congress and of the Committee of Safety; but placing himself under the protection of General Howe circa, 1776, he was attainted of high treason, forfeited his large estates—and thereupon went to England, deceasing in London, in 1825. William, the second son, was for a time a Lieutenant-Colonel in the Continental service. He also died a refugee loyalist abroad. James, a member of the Committee of Observation and Inspection for Pennsylvania, remained true to the cause of American Independence. He was furthermore the founder of Allentown, which place crystallized about Trout Hall on Jordan Creek (a summer seat of William Allen), subsequent to 1755. His property in and around that settlement, which for a half century and more fluctuated between the names of Allen's Town and Northampton (but now Allen*town*, although a bona-fide city), he devised to his daughters, to wit: Mrs. Greenleaf, Mrs. Tilghman and Mrs. Livingston. James Allen died in Philadelphia, in 1777. The townships of Allen and East Allen jointly with the aforementioned city (which should simply be called *Allen*,—neither more nor less), perpetuate the name of the enterprising founder of old Northampton County.

* Mr. Irish, who was commissioned a Justice of the Peace for the

who dispensed equity at his house, when not grinding grist in his mill, near the outlet of Saucon creek, two short miles lower down the West Branch of Delaware. Stating his case to the law-read miller, Ruetschi

County of Bucks, by Govenor Thomas, in April of 1741, bought lands near the mouth of the Saucon, at different times; the first purchase of 150 acres, bearing date of 12th April, 1738, on which day it was released to him by Casper Wistar, of the city of Philadelphia, brass button-maker, and Catharine, his wife. In 1743, he was possessed of upwards of 600 acres, all contiguous; these, together with the improvements including a mill (whose ruins are still standing in the rear of Mr. John Knecht's house in Shimersville), he conveyed in October of 1743 to George Cruikshank, of the Island of Montserrat, in the West Indies, sugar planter, who in his lifetime became lawfully seized in his desmesne as of fees of and in the amount of 900 acres of land, lying contiguous along Saucon Creek. Cruikshank, by his last will and testament—he deceased in March of 1746—devised this tract together with his New South Sea annuities, and his real estate in Montserrat to his children, James and Lathrop. But these divided the property in 1769,—whereupon, Lathrop, on marrying John Currie, of Reading, in the County of Berks, Esq., with her husband entered into possession of 450 acres, the homestead and the mill. In 1787, Currie deeded back to James Cruikshank, practitioner in physic, 180 acres, including the mill, the latter having meanwhile disposed of his moiety of the original bequest to Jesse Jones, yeoman, and to Felix Lynn, of Upper Saucon, practitioner in physic. James Cruikshank, of the village of Bethlehem, practitioner in physic, by his last will and testament dated 24th September, 1802, devised to Mary Currie, Francis Currie, and William Currie, children of John and Lathrop Currie, the aforementioned 180 acres and mill, both which, William Currie, of Plymouth township, in the County of Luzerne, yeoman, deeded to Jacob Shimer, of Bethlehem township, yeoman, in June of 1809, for $10,666.66 lawful money of the United States. Shimer's, now Knecht's mill, was built in 1812, and around it by way of nucleus, the brisk little village at the mouth of the Saucon, gradually grew.

adduced the nine points by way of fortifying his argument, urged his right of pre-emption, and concluded with a fair offer to purchase the lands in dispute, promising payment with undoubted security at an early day. Now had not Henry Antes,*—he resided at the time in that beautiful region of country, which stretches back of Pottstown, then called Falckner's swamp—a man versed in the law, and a warm friend of the Moravians, happened to be at Bethlehem on the 23d day of April, 1743 (which day marked the crisis in this feverish excitement about a strip of woodland in the wilderness), superintending the erec-

* Mr. Antes (he had immigrated prior to 1726, in which year he married Christiana De Wiesen, of White Marsh) was a highly respected citizen in his neighborhood, and a man of much influence with its German population, being esteemed alike for his integrity, and for his zeal in the cause of vital religion. His attachment to the Moravians dates back to the years in which Spangenberg (subsequently the presiding officer in the Bethlehem Economy) resided among the Schwenkfelders of Philadelphia County. With Count Zinzendorf he was on the most intimate terms, co-operating with him heartily in his attempt to unite the religiously inclined German element of the Province on an evangelical basis. Mr. Antes resided at Bethlehem, between June of 1745 and September of 1750, directing, meanwhile, the many improvements that were then being made at that place and at Nazareth. In December of 1745, he was commissioned a Justice of the Peace for the County of Bucks.

Mr. Antes died on his plantation in Falckner's Swamp, on the 20th July, 1755. John, a son, was a missionary of the Moravian Church, and an adventurous traveller in Egypt, between 1769 and 1781. Governor Simon Snyder, married for his second wife, Catharine, a daughter of Philip Frederic, oldest son of Henry and Christiana Antes.

tion of a much needed grist-mill (the same that became completely historical in the night of the 27th of January, 1870),—it is a question whether the future of the Simpson Tract would not have been altogether different from the one of which we are privileged to write,—and whether it would ever have boasted a royal crown. For Mr. Antes, on the aforementioned day, adjusted the difficulties between the contestants, in as far as his representations of the justice of the Moravian claim prevailed with Irish,—nay, even tempted the latter to the commission of an official act, when, at the close of their professional consultation in the dusty mill he insisted on serving a writ of ejectment on the squatter. In this extreme measure the peace-loving Moravians, however, refused to concur. Instead, they tolerated their discomfited rival, until such time as he could conveniently remove, and having compounded with him for his improvements entered into possession.

Three years subsequent to this piece of unpleasantness, William Allen and Margaret, his wife, made deed of this now historic piece of ground, to Jasper Payne, of Bethlehem, wine-cooper (a native of Twickenham, in the hundred of Isleworth, county of Middlesex O. E., "whose eel-pie house was for two centuries a favorite resort for refreshment and recreation to water-parties,"—but, in 1742 a resident of London, dwelling at the corner of Queen street and Watling street, St. Antholines), for the use and behoof of his Moravian Brethren, by indenture bearing date of 3d June, 1746, in consideration of the sum of 200*l.* lawful money of Pennsylvania,* to them well and truly paid, and under the yearly quitrent hereafter accruing to the chief lord of the fee. Its precise bearings and metes extracted from the field-works of Nicholas Scull, were these: "Beginning at a marked black-oak by the side of the West Branch of Delaware, opposite to an Island in the same" (vulgarly called Calypso Island, which was surveyed for Nathaniel Irish, in April of 1742, but transferred by him, in fee, to Henry Antes, in March of 1745, for 10*l.*, Pennsylvania currency,—but for the use of the Moravians, and thereupon patented by the three brothers Penn), "from thence extending by vacant land south twenty degrees west one hundred and sixty-two perches to a post; thence by the same east three hundred and thirteen perches to a post; thence by the same and William Allen's land north one hundred and seventy-four perches to a marked black-oak by the side of

* A sum equivalent to $533.33 United States money, reckoning 1*l.* extinct Pennsylvania currency equal to $2.66; at the rate, therefore, of $1.94 and the fraction of a hundredth per acre,—since which time, however, it may not be amiss to state, Simpson land in the due order of things, has materially advanced in price. Town lots in the borough of South Bethlehem, are being sold at this writing, at the rate of $9,000 per acre of land.

said river, and thence on the several courses thereof, to the place of beginning." *

So much of the history of the Simpson Tract from times immemorial (in which, in all probability fell its first tenure by the inevitable Indian), until the close of the squatter sovereignty of Conrad Ruetschi.

Having linked their newly-acquired possessions to the five hundred acre tract on which Bethlehem was being built, by means of a ferry (as was stated above), the Moravians set about bringing portions of them under cultivation. Such was the early and humble origin of the great Moravian farms on the south side of the Lehigh, which, ultimately, after the purchase of additional territory, numbered four, and were last known as the "Luckenbach Farm," the "Jacobi

---

* Although these terminal oaks have disappeared (whether they paid the debt of nature, or whether they fell victims to the cupidity of man, there are no means of ascertaining at this late day), and, although their lowlier brothers, the posts, have long since been removed,—yet by the aid of diverse drafts extant illustrating the successive purchases of lands by the Moravians in the vicinity of Bethlehem, it is not difficult to exactly locate the Simpson tract, obliterated as its ancient landmarks have been by the vicissitudes incident on time and tide. Beginning at the black-oak opposite the Island, its west line passes in the rear of the buildings of the Water Cure, and having cut Bishopthorpe in two, terminates at the edge of Tinsley Jeter's brick yard; from this point, the south line runs due east to a corner in the grounds of the Lehigh University, a few rods southeast of Packer Hall; thence the east line tends due north one hundred and seventy-four perches, striking the river's bank, a short distance below the New Street Bridge.

Farm," the Fuehrer Farm," and the Hoffert Farm." But of these, more hereafter.

Now to resume the thread of our narrative, the beginning of the Bethlehem ferry was on this wise: In midwinter, January 25th of 1743, a site for the much-needed convenience was selected, its southern terminus being a point on the river's bank immediately above the present railroad bridge, marked to this day by a group of sycamores, whose ancestors before them had shaded the first waterman who undertook to propel the ponderous flat across the swift-flowing Lehigh. His name, indeed, is lost, but it is recorded that the craft he navigated was drawn to the northern terminus of the ferry on the 11th day of March of the aforementioned year by eight horses, and successfully launched. But as the vessel was not christened, there was no breaking of bottles nor waste of wine. Furthermore, it is recorded, that in February of 1745, one Adam Schaus,* who was keeping a public house in a small

* Mr. Schaus, one of those historical personages frequently met with, who break through the clouds and darkness of the past only at intervals, or if you choose, play on the surface of its gloom fitfully as do ignes fatui over marsh or stagnant pool,—immigrated from Albsheim in the Lower Palatinate, with Barbarba, his wife, and Philip and Frederic, their sons, about 1735. He was a wheelwright by occupation, and was settled in Falkner's Swamp, when in December of 1741, he made the acquaintance of Count Zinzendorf, by whom he was introduced to the favorable notice of the Moravians. Being a man of good parts, we need not be surprised to learn that he was ap-

way on the Ysselstein plantation hard by, consented to conduct the ferry for his Moravian friends. This he did for almost a twelvemonth, and then accepted an appointment to act as miller at the Bethlehem mill.

Meanwhile the question of erecting a house of entertainment for the accommodation of travellers, at some point in their territory, had been agitated by the people of Bethlehem, it having been found that the steady march of settlement northwards into the Forks was converting their quiet villiage into a thoroughfare, and making it a halting-place, at times for idle and impertinent intruders. The arrangements in their large

---

pointed to act as secretary for an ecclesiastical convention (one of a series of seven), which sat in the house of George Huebner, a Schwenkfelder, in the Swamp, in January following. About this time the Count loaned Mr. Schaus 50*l.*, on terms, that would nowadays be called easy, as the debt was not liquidated as late as July of 1745. In the spring of 1743, the subject of these memoirs tarried some time at Bethlehem, as he and his son Philip had been engaged to assist Mr. Antes in erecting and putting into running order a grist-mill. Soon after its completion, he removed his family into Saucon township, in the immediate vicinity of that place. Here he opened a house of entertainment, in which in December of 1744, a third son was born to him, named Gottlieb. Subsequently he removed to Bethlehem, as is stated above, and was manifestly a member of its Economy, as in August of 1745, its steward supplied him with "a frock and breeches made of linen without lining," valued at 5 shillings. Subsequent to Mr. Schaus' retirement from the mill, his history grows obscure; yet there is reason for believing that after the erection of the new county-town in the Forks, he sought to better

houses (and others, there were none) forbade the lodging of strangers among them, save at much inconvenience;—and an Inn within the precincts of the town, it was argued, would merely invite invidious comment on the part of the public, which was determined to remain ignorant of their object and aim. In fact, it was already at that time reported that the Moravians were a monastic order, that their houses were convents, and that at Bethlehem "the glimmering tapers shed forth light on cowled heads, and the nuns' sweet hymn was heard sung low in the dim mysterious aisle," No wonder, then, it was deemed expedient to locate the proposed Inn on the Simpson Tract. Ac-

---

his fortunes there, in the whirl of business, which, it was hoped by men of sanguine temperament, would attend its growth and development as a seat of Justice, and a centre of inland commerce. So much is certain, however, that in 1760, both Adam and Frederic Schaus were residents of Easton; the former a landlord, the latter a mason, and superintending too the work on the Moravian house, then in course of erection in that place. It would furthermore appear that the son succeeded the father; for it is said that in Frederic Schaus' Tavern, the Honorable the Court occasionally sat in conclave prior to the completion of the Court-house in the spring of 1766. Further than these, there are no reliable notices of the Schaus family as far as this history is concerned; yet, it may be stated, that its modern branches write *Shouse* upon their hereditary escutcheon. Finally, Adam Schaus was never landlord of the Crown Inn, the statement to that effect made by writers of its history, being an erroneous deduction based upon allusions to his keeping a house of entertainment over against Bethlehem; which point we hope this narrative will definitely settle.

cordingly, in the early spring of 1745, an eligible site was selected at a point a few rods east of the terminus of the ferry, on high ground near the river's bank. Work was thereupon commenced; but as the time and attention of the industrious little community were neccessarily occupied with the labors of the farm and the shops, also, it was late in the summer before the house was habitable. There, then, it stood in September of 1745, in a small clearing in the woods,—as to its exterior, a rather imposing-looking structure, forty by twenty-eight feet more or less, compactly knit together from white-oak logs, with two stories and a high gable-roof,—as to its interior, however, having four rooms in each story, all floored with one and a half-inch white-oak plank; the studding of the partition-walls being posts of the same material, grooved so as to receive cross pieces, with a snug filling of cut straw and clay; the casing of the doors and windows, moreover, worked to the very beads and fluting from solid timbers; wooden latches and bolts, with not a nail in the carpentering but what had been wrought from well-qualified horseshoes by the nailsmith at Bethlehem. It should not surprise us, such being the case, that the sturdy house was found sound to the core in the year of its demolition, which was the one hundred and thirteenth after its erection.

It may in the next place, be well to acquaint the

THE CROWN INN, 1757.

South Front—From "A view of Bethlehem, one of the Brethren's principal settlements in Pennsylvania," drawn by Nicholas Garrison, and published November 24th, 1757.

reader with the lines of travel from which it was expected the young Inn would draw its annual revenue,—partially, at least. Now the point it occupied with respect to these, was reasonably strategic, as will become evident from a glance at any map of the then settled portions of the Province, which shows the following to have been the system of roads adopted in the Forks of Delaware. There was, in the first place, the great King's Road from the capital. This had been stretching northward by easy stages ever since the days of William Penn, when, in 1738, another link was added to its important chain, it being in that year extended "from Thomas Morris' road in Perkasie,"* to Nathaniel Irish's stone quarry (a point in the old Hellertown road† at Iron Hill). But in March of 1745, at the very time when the building of the Inn was in its inception, the inhabitants of Naza-

* The Manor of Perkasie or Perkasea, was a tract of 10,000 acres of land, lying within the limits of Hilltown and Rockhill townships, Bucks County, granted by William Penn to Samuel Carpenter, Edward Penington and Isaac Norris, by letters patent bearing date of 25th October, 1701. In 1735, the three grantees conveyed the tract to John Penn the first, when it became known by the name of "John Penn's Manor of Perkasea, in the County of Bucks." In July of 1759, Thomas Penn donated one-fourth of the estate to the University of Pennsylvania.

† William Bradford, in a pamphlet entitled "An Account of distances from the City of Philadelphia of all the places of note in the improved parts of the Province," published in 1755, gives the follow-

reth and Bethlehem, with others, humbly petitioned the worshipful Court of Justices holden at Newtown in the County of Bucks, praying in these words, to wit.: "that they may have a road fit for wagons to pass from Saucon mill to Bethlehem and thence to Nazareth, on account of a corn-mill that is at Bethlehem, without which road the people of Nazareth, and other the inhabitants of the county will be put to great inconvenience, and the same mill to them be rendered useless." Hereupon the desired road was laid out

---

ing points of interest in the old King's Road, and their precise distances from the Court-house.

From the Court-house to Bethlehem, viz.:

	Miles.	Qrs.	Perches.
To Poole's Bridge,	—	2	65
" Norris',	2	1	37
" Farmhill Meeting,	2	3	35
" Rising Sun,	3	2	40
" Stenton,	5	1	—
" Germantown Meeting-house,	6	1	30
" Mount Airy,	8	2	52
" Scull's,	10	—	22
" Ottinger's,	12	2	35
" Francis',	12	3	38
" White Marsh Church,	13	1	33
" Benjamin Davis',	16	—	54
" Baptist Meeting,	23	1	57
" Housekeeper's,	25	1	57
" Swamp Meeting,	37	2	47
" Stoffel Wagner's,	47	2	—
" Bethlehem,	52	3	57

as follows, "beginning at Irish's stone quarry at a white-oak, thence northwest forty degrees north thirty-five perches; thence west northwest one hundred perches; thence west sixty-nine perches; thence west northwest one hundred and fifty perches to Ysselstein's plantation; thence north over the river Lecha* ninety-three perches; thence west northwest one hundred and fifty-eight perches to the Bethlehem lane; thence west one hundred and twenty perches to the mill; and from the Bethlehem line north northeast quite to Nazareth twenty-eight hundred and forty perches." Beyond that hamlet there was close connection by bridle-paths with Depui's settlement in the Minisinks, which, in turn, was tapped by the historic "Mine Road" that led you through the valley of the Mamakating to Kingston in Esopus. A few days' labor it will be conceded, would suffice to cut a way from the Inn through the woods to the Indian ford.

*By way of an old Indian ford, which Heckerwelder states to have been in the great trail leading northward from the lower country of the Delawares, even from the mouth of their national river,—said trail on crossing the Lecha-wiech-ink forking off in different directions to the scattered towns of the Lennape, in inland Pennsylvania,—as far west as the Alleghenies. This ancient ford crossed the Lehigh on Ysselstein's plantation, bearing according to an actual survey, north 11 degrees west to the head of Ysselstein's Island (the island now held by the Bethlehem Iron Company), thence 15 degrees east to the left bank, measuring 58 perches from shore to shore.

There was, in the second place a high road to Martin's Ferry over Delaware in the exact fork of that river, which road had been petitioned for in the same year 1745, by one David Martin, of Trentown, who six years prior had obtained "a grant and patent with the privilege of keeping a ferry from the Pennsylvania shore to the upper end of an island called Tinicum, to the place in the county of Morris in West Jersey, called Marble Mountain." Thus the Bethlehem Inn was also on the line of travel from New York. In the third place a bridle path (converted into a highway* in 1760) struck southwesterly from the house over the Lehigh hills towards the German settlements in Macungy,—another due west to Solomon Jennings' plantation, and diverse others north and northwest to the seats of the Ulster-Scots on Menagassi and the springs of Calisuck. Finally there was a second ford of the river connecting with "the road through Bethlehem to Philadelphia," bearing from said road first south by east, next due south, and next south southwest across the river, measuring thirty-four perches from shore to shore by actual

*This road, called the "road to Salisbury" on olden drafts, and subsequent to 1761, "the Emmaus Road," as late as 1826, forked from the Philadelphia Road near the bridge, thence passing up the hill through the grounds of E. P. Wilbur and John Smylie, Jr., and onward south by west as far as Foelkner's butchery, at which point it struck the present road.

survey. What more eligible site than this for a house of entertainment? And yet the one of which we are privileged to write, turned its face modestly from the garish glare of dusty highways towards the beautiful mountain, borrowing quiet from its peaceful calm, bloom from the roses that suffused its bosom at dawn and eventide, and nut-brown health from the flood of sunlight in which it bathed on its southern lookout, day after day during its lifetime as an Inn, which numbered forty-nine long years. Meanwhile its back, we must confess, was turned indecorously upon Bethlehem.

Fifteen landlords, to whom it is now proposed to introduce the reader in turn, presided over the fortunes of the house thus auspicioulsy established, in the interval between September of 1745 and October of 1794,—said housc bcing at first very appropriatcly and without ought of affectation called by the Moravians of Bethlehem, "The Tavern over ye water,"—but by others "The Tavern near Bethlehem," or "The Bethlehem Tavern."

Now the names of these olden worthies, recited in the order of their succession, are the following, to wit: Samuel Powell, Frederic Hartmann, Jobst Vollert, Hartman Verdriess, John Leighton, John Godfrey Grabs, John Nicholas Schaeffer, Ephraim Culver, Andreas Horne, John Lischer, Ephraim Culver (a second time), Augustus H. Francke,

Valentine Fuehrer, John G. Stoll and George Schindler.*

On the 30th September 1745, Samuel Powell a native of Whitchurch (*Album Monasterium*), a market-town in the Whitchurch division of the hundred of North Bradford, County of Salop, brazier, —(he immigrated in June of 1742 and since then had resided in Philadelphia) and Martha, his wife, occupied the Inn, which, during their incumbency (it expired on the 31st of May 1746), after having been warmed and duly furnished, sustained the character of a very sober and orderly house. In fact, having been granted neither permit nor license, it was a house of entertainment in the restricted acceptation of the term only,—proving, nevertheless, a useful acquisition for the Moravian settlement, in as far as upwards of two-hundred visitors were booked at Bethlehem, for the eight months of the Powell administration.†

*The editor of the Memorials of the Moravian Church states erroneously (see page 262, Vol. 1), that one Anthony Gilbert was a landlord of the old Crown Inn. He was led to a committal of this error by obscure allusions to said Gilbert as keeping a house of entertainment, called The Crown, in 1745—which house, however, he has since satisfactorily located in Germantown. It might repay some antiquary to institute researches so as to develop the history of the hostelry in that ancient town, the honored namesake of the one of which these pages treat.

†Samuel Powell died at Philadelphia, 10th September, 1762, and was buried in Potter's Field, now Washington Square.

The Powells were succeeded by Frederic Hartmann and Margaret his wife, both of whom had immigrated in the interval between 1725 and 1740, a period of time unprecedentedly rich in the influx of Palatines into the Province,—they being not unlikely included in the number of those of whom Secretary Logan writes to the Proprietaries so excitedly—"they come in crowds, go to the best vacant tracts and seize upon them as places of common spoil. But when they are sought out and challenged for the right of occupancy, these Germans allege it was published in Europe that we desired and solicited colonists and had a superabundance of land, and therefore they had come with no means to pay." Be this as it may, Mr. Hartmann was residing in the vicinity of the Simpson Tract when he accepted the appointment to the Inn. In anticipation of his accession as landlord, the house, meanwhile, had been well furnished with all that is indispensable to an Inn, besides the appurtenances of a dairy. This appears from the following record; viz.:

"19 May 1746. Tavern over ye water Dr., for Sundries, to wit: Two cows 7*l.*, one churn 3*s.*—one quart wine-measure, one pint do, one half pint do, one gill do, one half-gill do, all of pewter, and three gill and two dram-glasses 1*l.* — two hogsheads of cider 3*l.*—four casks do 2*l.* 5*s.*—one cask of metheglin 17*s.* 6*d.*—a small cupboard with an iron lock 8*s.*—one walnut table 16*s.*—a tin funnel, an iron strainer, a beef-fork and a ladle 4*s.* 6*d.*—two iron candlesticks 1*s.* 6*d.*—six pewter plates 10*s.*—twelve pewter spoons 5*s.* 6*d.* and two soup dishes 12*s.*—" Subsequently, in this administration, the chambers were furnished with green rugs and blankets, and net-work window curtains. Two handsome brass candlesticks were provided for the sitting-room, and the kitchen's outfit completed by the addition of six black-handled knives and forks, one copper coffee-pot, one gridiron for broils, one pewter tea-pot, and three brown cups and three saucers of china. Thus Mr. Hartmann was enabled to offer right royal cheer and goodly creature-comforts to tired travellers, at the house standing on Simpson land, which was worth scarce fifteen shillings per acre in the market; his rates were reasonable, too—to wit: fourpence for a breakfast of tea or coffee; sixpence for a dinner; (but eightpence, for a dinner, with a pint of beer;) fourpence, for a supper, cold; sixpence for ditto, hot; twopence for a night's lodging; and twelvepence for a night's hay and oats, for a horse.

Meanwhile, however, steps had been taken to have the Inn established upon a legal basis. For this purpose the Court of Quarter Sessions of the

Peace, holden at Newtown* in June of 1746, was duly petitioned for a license, and a bond having been given to Lawrence Growdon, Esq., his Worship on the bench,—that solemn body forthwith allowed and licensed Frederic Hartmann to sell beer and cider by small measure in the township of Saucon, in the County of Bucks, until the 24th of June next ensuing,—he promising to observe the laws and ordinances of the Province which were or should be made relating to retailers of beer and cider by small measure. By this process our Inn was transformed into a house of entertainment, in a more popular acception of the term than before.

The net income of the Tavern for the seven months between the 19th May and the 31st December 1746, amounted to 26*l.* 9*s.* 1*d.*, a result which indicates that its management was efficient as well as acceptable. But on the 12th of January 1747, the landlady (she was a native of the ancient city of Worms in the Rhineland) died—and not three months after her interment in the new grave-yard†

* The ancient village of Newtown, situated on a small branch of the Neshaminy, ten miles northwest from Bristol, was the first seat of Justice of the County of Bucks, whither its inhabitants repaired for legal business even from regions as remote as the Minisinks, until the erection of Northampton County and the establishment of a Court at Easton in June of 1752.

† Almost forgotten, as all traces of its existence have long since been obliterated, is the burial place which the early Moravians provided for

on the Simpson Tract, Mr. Hartmann retired from the Inn. We are inclined to believe that he died subsequent to 1756 at Nazareth.*

---

the settlers residing immediately south of the Lehigh, with whom they were connected by the ties of religion. A draft of "Bethlehem Lands," lying on that bank of the river, drawn in 1757, locates the graveyard on rising ground, some thirty rods due south from the "great spring,"—therefore near the intersection of Ottawa and Second Street—and shows it to have been a small enclosure in the very heart of the primitive woods, which at that time were unbroken as far east as the line of the road then leading to Emmaus. There are nineteen official records of interments made in it between the 12th of January 1747, and the 9th of October, 1767. Well authenticated tradition, however, states, that while the Continental Hospital occupied Bethlehem, its sick were occasionally billeted in the farm-houses and in the Inn on the Simpson Tract, and that a number of Revolutionary soldiers were interred in the forsaken grave-yard, as well as in trenches dug in the fields. It is said, furthermore, that the spot was plowed over in the early part of the century, —and even old inhabitants who were once familiar with its site are no longer able to fix its precise locality, so completely have ancient landmarks been removed or disappeared. (See Appendix for further notice of the grave-yard on the Simpson Tract.)

* This history would be incomplete, were no mention made of one Andrew Ostrom and Jane his wife (they immigrated from London in the autumn of 1743), who took apartments at the Inn in October of 1746, awaiting the completion of a house then in the course of erection for them on a tract of thirty acres, situated on the mountain over against the head of the upper island, which tract Ostrom had taken up on warrant, the three Penns confirming the same to him by patent in November of 1760. Jane Ostrom died on "the Ridge" in December of 1758, and was buried in the grave-yard on the Simpson Tract. In 1764 Ostrom conveyed his land to the Moravians. In 1853 it was sold to Chas. W. Rauch of Bethlehem. The inexhaustible quarry of Potsdam sandstone which underlies Ostrom's Ridge, furnished the

It was a fortunate circumstance that at this juncture there was a person on the spot who was well fitted, and willing to assume the responsibilities of a landlord, and thus to fill the vacancy created by Mr. Hartmann's resignation. This person was one Jobst Vollert, of whose history we know the following: In the early summer of 1746, Jobst, and Mary Elizabeth, née Miller (she was a sister of Daniel Miller of Philadelphia, potter), his wife, removed with their family to Bethlehem from their late residence on the Schuylkill in Coventry township in the County of Chester. There they had become acquainted with Moravian itinerants, and attached to the Moravian Society. But as there was no dwelling to let in the infant settlement, several apartments in our Inn were assigned to Jobst, at a rent of fifty shillings per annum, he stipulating at the same time "to teach James to read and write in consideration of his wood, which wood said James* is to split." Mr. Vollert entered

material of the old Bethlehem buckwheat-mill erected in 176(, of the Bethlehem Iron Company's buildings, and of those of the Lehigh University.

* It is highly probable that "James" who is here woven into the web of this history (he was errand-boy and hostler at the Inn), is the same who inevitably brings up the rear as often as an enumeration is made of the Moravians who immigrated into the Province from Georgia in April of 1740. In 1747 James was transferred to Nazareth, where we lose sight of him.

the Inn on these terms on the 17th of June, 1746, and thereupon commenced his career as an educator. Now, having been the first of that ancient and honorable order who resided on the south bank of Lecha, which in our day (such has been the onward march of civilization) abounds in men and women of letters,—and having moreover left a noble record and an inspiriting example of disinterestedness in his calling, it would not only not be undignified but highly proper, for one or another, or for all of the institutions of learning on the Simpson Tract, to confer a degree upon the memory of old Jobst Vollert, and to inscribe his name on their rolls of honor.

Right pleasantly, then, we doubt not, occupied with his pupil, with enunciation, stress, pot-hooks and hangers, did the long months of the winter of 1746 and 1747 pass—spring opened, the trees gave signs of life, and when the weir in the Lehigh had been repaired, and the first shad of the season were being taken, Jobst Vollert succeeded to the Inn,—he being the third landlord in the succession. We much regret our inability to adduce a single occurrence of interest as having transpired during this brief incumbency, either at the Inn or upon its premises; but the opening of a boarding-school on the 25th day of May, 1747, in the "Behringer House"—(it stood not a stone's throw east from the foot of the stairway by which you descend from the New Street bridge), is an event whose significance claims for it more than a passing notice. The great doctors of Geology tell us, that each period in that immensity of time in which they revel, produced some form of life prophetic of some nobler kindred form of life destined to appear in a succeeding age—a law, whose application here will invest the genesis of the school in the "Behringer House" with extraordinary import,—demonstrating it to have been prophetic of those higher scholastic creations which shine resplendent in our day,—the imperial University, the academic shades of Melrose and Penrose, and sweet Bishopthorpe in fairyland. In another respect, also, the school which has thus been introduced to the reader's notice, was geological in character — it having had epochs, each of which was sharply defined by the introduction of a different order of beings. From the day of its organization to the 10th day of January, 1749, it was occupied by lads, the major part of whom had, prior to the first mentioned date, been inmates of a similar institution, conducted under the auspices of the Moravian Society, at some obscure point in the Long Swamp. These boys have come down to us with no good record, it must be confessed, it being said of them that they were unruly spirits and needed disciplining. We can find no clew, however, to the standing with their contemporaries of the girls or young lasses who took possession of the premises in May of 1749, — but on their evacuating them in December of 1753, the "Behringer House" was converted into a hattery, probably because the neighborhood abounded in rabbits, the fur of which animals was fabricated into the styles of felt-hats worn by the gentlemen of that day. On a draft of lands lying on the south bank of Lecha, drawn in 1757, the old school-house no longer appears.

To return to Jobst Vollert. On the 2d of November, 1747, he retired from the Inn, and removed with his family to a plantation of eighty-one acres, lying south and southwest of the Simpson Tract, which he had purchased of one Tobias Weber, a Lutheran, last from Germantown. The house stood on the road to Macungy, and had been built by Weber in February of 1744.* In September of 1754, Vollert added one hundred and fourteen acres and one half acre of mountain land to his domain, these having been exposed for sale at public outcry by Nicholas Scull, then Sheriff of the County of Northampton, as the property of one Anthony

*Its site was at the crossing of the run which springs in the Salisbury hills, and which, after passing in the rear of the Church of the Nativity, struggles through the improvements of South Bethlehem to find its old outlet into the Lehigh, east of the Union Depot.

Albrecht (he had been imported in October of 1732, in the pink John and William of Sunderland, Constable Tymperton, master, from Rotterdam, but last from Dover as by clearance thence), from Mannheim, baker. But the "Albrecht Farm" stretched from the south line of the "Weber Tract" upwards to the very crest of the mountain, and was well-paved with syenite, garnished profusely with vaccinia, and rich in ruffed and pinnated grouse. In August of 1755, these two plantations passed into the hands of the Moravians, and in the following May, Jobst Vollert removed to Easton, where we find him, in the autumn of 1760, assisting John Bosch, carpenter, Frederick Schaus, mason, and Abraham Berlin, blacksmith, in erecting a large dwelling for the Moravians, on a lot "bounded east by Pomfret street, south by lot No. 120 — west by a twenty-foot alley, and north by Ferry street." While in the act of digging a well on these premises,—the curtain falls upon Jobst and we fail to recognise him elsewhere on the stage of history.

On the third of November, 1747, Hartmann Verdriess (Vandriess), last from Carter's Run in Warwick township, Lancaster County, miller, and Ann Catharine, née Bender (she had immigrated in her bellehood with her parents from Heilbrunn, in the Palatinate, and had settled in Conestoga) his wife, occupied the Bethlehem Tavern, as host and hostess, they being the fourth couple called to administer its concerns. But their career was brief, — and even in its tenor, closing on the 29th day of March, 1748. Elsewhere, however, Mr. Verdriess made his mark. He was twice miller at the Friedensthal mill, on Lehietan, touching the Barony of Nazareth on the east,—and was landlord of "The Rose" hard by, between August of 1756 and April of 1759, at a time when living in the bush was fraught with perils, as white men's scalps were at a premium in the Indian market. His experiences during that period of his life are fully rehearsed in "A Red Rose from the Olden Time;"*—hence, passing them over thus lightly, we proceed to state, that in 1766 Mr. and Mrs. Verdriess removed their family beyond Mason and Dixon's line (about the time when these distinguished mathematicians and astronomers had reached the summit of the Little Allegheny in their historic survey), and seated themselves in Frederic County, Maryland, adjacent to a Moravian settlement (since 1785 called Graceham), then growing upon a small tract of land, which Frederic, the last Lord Baltimore had patented to those people in November of 1751. Here Mr. Verdriess died in 1774. His widow, however, returned to Bethlehem,

* "Or, A Ramble through the Annals of the Rose Inn, on the Barony of Nazareth in the days of the Province." Small 4to pp. 50. King and Baird, Printers, Philadelphia.

where she died in April of 1801. Peter Verdriess, a grandson, was an eminent classical teacher in Philadelphia between 1815 and 1825.

John Leighton, a native of the seaport of Dundee, in the town of Forfarshire, Scotland, but last from Lamb's Inn (Broad Oak), a Moravian settlement in the County of Essex, O. E., baker, and Sarah, m. n. Clifford, born in the ancient city of Canterbury (*Durovernum*), both of whom had immigrated in the autumn of 1743 with one hundred and fifteen others, (they sailed in the Moravian ship "The Little Strength") took charge of the hostelry on the 29th of March, 1748. Their administration of its affairs was, upon the whole, a prosperous one,—the house netting 63*l.* 2*s.* 9¼*d.* in 1749—71*l.* 16*s.* 7½*d.* in 1750—and 88*l.* 11*s.* 3*d.* for the year ending 26th July, 1752,—although beer and cider were the only beverages dispensed.* Governor Hamilton honored the Inn a few

* Fortunately there is extant and in good keeping, a view of Bethlehem from the declivity of the mountain, taken by some unknown limner in 1751, in which the Inn, as far as it occupies a position in the foreground, looks us full in the face. We need no further testimony than what is furnished by this ancient drawing, that the entrance to the hostelry was from the south, and that there was no signboard as yet to arrest the attention of the passing traveller. For the rest, the house is of imposing appearance, comparatively speaking, and its surroundings such as are usually presented by a clearing only recently hewn out of a primitive wilderness. To give life to this picture, the artist introduces two figures;—one, a female with pitcher in hand passing out of the

moments by his presence on the 13th of July 1752, while on his way to Easton to confer with Mr. Parsons* on matters touching the welfare and dignity of the newly erected seat of Justice. There was at this time a great want of highways through the Counties of Bucks and Northampton to said seat of Justice, and as John Chapman and John Watson, surveyors, had not yet laid out "a commodious road from the mouth of the West Branch of Delaware opposite the town of Easton (the landing place of a well-accustomed ferry over Delaware River), over the aforementioned West Branch into the great road leading from Saucon to the City of Philadelphia,"—(lately asked for by divers the inhabitants of the County of Northampton)—the Governor was

---

door—and the other, an Indian, seated on a log, near the well at which the damsel purposes to fill her vessel.

* William Parsons, who rocked Easton in her cradle and watched over her infant footsteps with paternal solicitude, was probably a native of England. We find him residing in Philadelphia prior to 1722 (in that year he married), a shoemaker by trade, and a member of Franklin's Junta Club in which he passed for "a man having a profound knowledge of mathematics." About 1743 he was appointed their Surveyor General by the Penns. Ill health compelling him to resign this laborious position in June of 1748, he thereupon removed to Lancaster, whence he was summoned by the Proprietaries in the autumn of 1752 to fill the offices in the seat of Justice of the newly erected County of Northampton. He died at Easton in December of 1757. Several of his daughters united with the Moravians. His widow, who removed to Bethlehem in 1769, died there in March of 1773.

necessitated to take a circuitous route to reach his destination. This brought him to our Inn. But, eighteen days after his Honor and his Honor's suite had refreshed themselves with beer and cider at Leighton's, — the worthy couple retired from public life. Mr. Leighton died at Bethlehem in August of 1756. His widow survived him till in April of 1785.

Although there was as yet no farm on the tract with whose history this writing is concerned, portions of it had, meanwhile, been brought under cultivation, and in 1747 a barn was erected near the Inn, in order to obviate the inconvenience of ferrying the hay and fodder over the river to the Economy's farm-yard in Bethlehem, — and also to permit of housing such kine as were pastured on its south bank. There being plentiful subsistence for sheep in the grassy swales in the lowland, the Economy's entire flock (it numbered in the aforementioned year two hundred and seventy head, including one hundred and ten ewes and lambs from the Barony) was summered on the Simpson Tract annually. One John Godfrey Grabs, a native of wool-growing Silesia (he and his wife Ann Mary had immigrated with a large colony in November of 1743, most of whose members had been brought over for the special purpose of reclaiming the Barony from the wilderness, — these, therefore, being the pioneers who felled its primitive forests, enriched its water-courses with made meadows, and sowed its sunny uplands with wheat and rye, until at five distinct points its acres smiled with the gifts of Ceres, and eventually, Nazareth, Sicily-like, became the granary of a Republic) — was duly appointed shepherd. This appointment was dictated by prudence, as the wolves had not yet deserted their ancestral homes in the neighborhood. It was for Grabs to guard the flock against harm from these hungry denizens of the bush,—whether seated under the shade of some oak or chestnut, or whether in his two-wheeled lodge on inclement days, while beguiling his tedious watch, not with foolish reed or oaten pipe, but with knitting stout hosen from the wool of his own growing. Nevertheless, it happened occasionally, that a wolf or two, bolder than their fellows, would dog the tracks of some inexperienced lamb or yearling, and dispensing with the hypocritical sophistry of their kinsman in Æsop, despatch it summarily, while in the very act of drinking at the run half way up the mountain. This, then, was the idyllic epoch in the past of the Simpson Tract, a veritable return to the days of poetry and fable, — twin-sisters in the realm of letters. It is true there were no Phyllises at hand, (save the lasses at school in the "Behringer House")—but Mr. Grabs, who has shown himself a utilitarian and no dreamer, we venture to say, was proof against their harmless little ways. Be this as it may, a well authenticated tradition, asserts that the unruly lads occasionally wheeled the shepherd's lodge into the river, when he was called from his post to follow his fleecy charge in their wayward movements through the valley. While a knowledge of these vagaries may serve to detract from the perfection of the idyl we were called upon to delineate, it distracts not a whit from our acquaintance with the instincts of human nature.*

It was from this pastoral occupation that Mr. Grabs was promoted to the Inn on the 26th day of July 1752, it being precisely two months after sheep-shearing. He and his wife were the sixth couple incumbent, and stood at its head for almost four years. Before proceeding to review the great events in this administration, it becomes us to acquaint the reader with the following occurrences of minor importance. And first our Inn was invested with new powers, when in the autumn of 1753, there were displayed in its tap-room the following letters patent:

"Whereas John Godfrey Grabs hath been recommended unto me as a sober and fit person to keep a house of entertainment, and being requested to grant him a license for the same, I do hereby license and

* It may prove interesting to some reader to learn that Casper Beckel, John Salterbach, Christopher Demuth and John Brodhead (a son of Daniel Brodhead of the Minisinks) were the last inmates of this school.

allow the said John Godfrey Grabs to keep a public house in the township of Saucon over against Bethlehem in the County of Northampton, for the selling of wine, rum, punch and other spirituous liquors, until the 17th day of August next; Provided, he shall not, at any time in the said term suffer any drunkenness, unlawful gaming, or any other disorders, or sell any drink to the Indians to debauch or hurt them; but in all things observe and practice all laws and ordinances of this Government to his said employment relating.

"Given under my hand and seal-at-arms, the 17th day of August, in the 27th year of our Sovereign Lord and King George the Second, and in the year of our Lord one thousand seven hundred and fifty three.

Signed JAMES HAMILTON."

[L. S.]

Hereupon, for some reason nowhere given, the income of the house markedly increased, its profits for the interval between the aforecited instrument and the close of the year being 34*l.*, and for the year ending 31st December 1754, 247*l.* 10*s.* 6*d.*

The cost of the annual licenses issued, as was customary in those times, by the Honorable the Governor, on recommendation of the Court of General Quarter Sessions of the Peace, was 2*l.* 5*s.* 9*d.*, for the years 1755 and 1756.

A new era was now about to dawn upon the Province and our Inn, in the course of which the latter was reluctantly drawn out of its cherished seclusion by being subjected to distasteful publicity, was closely linked in its fortunes to the former, and was brought face to face with the great actors of the bloody drama, the scene of which was destined to be laid on the frontiers of Pennsylvania. French ambition and French aggression provoked the first war, in which the followers of William Penn engaged with the aborigines. Whatever other considerations may have moved the Indians to entertain unfriendly feelings towards the descendants of a man whose memory they revered, whether loss of confidence in their integrity, or a sense of injury, or a wild hope of regaining their ancestral seats,— it is a question whether they would have followed up these feelings by acts of open hostility, had they not been incited by the insidious representations of the French of Canada. An alliance with the Indian tribes of the Province, the latter well knew would enable them to carry on their military operations in the Ohio country successfully, and to realize their schemes of territorial aggrandizement. In this way, then, were the Delaware nation and lesser tribes, residing on the Susquehanna and eastward, seduced from their allegiance to the British crown, and led to inflict much suffering upon the white settlements which stretched along the line of the Keck-achtany or Endless Mountains, from the romantic point at which the Delaware has broken their barrier, to the valley of the Conococheague, on the confines of Maryland. Passing over the occupation of Presque Isle (Erie) by the French in 1749, their advance to Venango, and the subsequent erection of Fort Duquesne in the Forks of the Kit-hanne or Alleghany, we come to the memorable attempt made by the English to dislodge the invaders from this stronghold, and drive them back to their legitimate seats on the St. Lawrence. Braddock's defeat on Frazier's run, near the banks of the Monongahela, on the 9th of July, 1755, was not only a fatal termination of a campaign which it had been hoped would inflict a decisive blow upon the enemy, but proved the direct means of encouraging the disaffected Indians to make the frontiers of the Province the scene of a predatory warfare, in which the northern bounds of old Northampton were severely scourged at intervals during a period of almost three years.

With the movements of the savages in this quarter, only, are we here concerned, and in briefly reviewing their course, we would state that the massacre at the Gnadenhutten mission (Lehighton), on the evening of the 24th of November, 1755, was the first indication given to the inhabitants of that

County that the enemy was at their doors. Its remoter settlements, and among these the scattered plantations that nestled in the small valleys immediately north of the Blue Mountain, drained by the Pocopoco and its branches, the Analomink, McMichael's and the Cherry Creek,—and the Pennsylvania Minisinks, suffered most severely in the winter of 1755 and 1756. So emboldened were the savages grown in consequence of their successful forays, that in January of the last mentioned year, their scalp-yell was heard within the precincts of the Barony of Nazareth, and Bethlehem was only saved from destruction at their hands by the exercise of extreme prudence, and by incessant watchfulness on the part of its inhabitants.

The fear which now seized upon the dwellers on the frontiers is indescribable; and as Government moved slowly in devising means for their protection (it was the middle of December of 1755, when Franklin, who had been prevailed upon to take charge of the northen frontier, and to provide for the defence of the inhabitants by raising troops and building a line of forts, moved to the seat of war), they placed their safety in flight. In this way it came to pass, that within six weeks after the first inroads of the enemy, not only was transmontane Northampton almost entirely deserted by the whites, but even the plantations in the tier of townships resting against the eastern slope of the Blue Mountain were left to their fate,—invariably the torch of the Indian warrior. It was in this precipitate hegira now, that the Moravian farms and villages were sought out by the fugitives, and were thus converted into cities of refuge,—and some of them, moreover, into rude strongholds, girt with palisades, after the fashion of those times of primitive warfare. This condition of things reached its climax, it is true, in the early winter of 1756; nevertheless, even pending negotiations for peace with the Indians (there were three conferences held with them at Easton alone, in the interval between July of 1756 and August of 1757), there occurred repetitions of the horrors which had marked the inception of hostilities. At a treaty made between Governor Denny and the Delaware King Tadeuskundt, at Easton, in August of 1757, a peace was finally confirmed.

Meanwhile, the Bethlehem Tavern had been the scene of lesser acts in the exciting drama of the day. Its precincts were crowded with fugitives in December of 1755. Landlord Grabs scarcely knew how to provide for these destitute people.* Standing, furthermore in the highway of travel between

* Elizabeth, the wife of Solomon Davis, a refugee from Allen township, died at the Inn on the 25th of January, 1756, and was buried in the grave-yard near by.

Fort Allen* (Weissport) and Easton — between an important military outpost, and the point which had been selected by the Indians as the place of conference, it will not surprise us to learn that it was occasionally a rendezvous for the soldiery in the Province service, and frequently the halting-place of the disaffected Delawares and their dusky allies. The following events occurred at the Inn during the last months of Grabs' incumbency.

---

*This was the second stronghold in a cordon of stockades erected along the line of the Blue Mountain, between the Delaware and the Susquehanna. It was built under Franklin's direction, on the left bank of the Lehigh, at a point where Col. Jacob Weiss commenced Weissport in 1785; was completed on the 25th of January, 1756, and named in honor of Chief Justice William Allen. The well in the stockade may be seen on the premises of the Fort Allen House. It should be carefully preserved, not only because it is a memorial of the old Indian War, but also because it testifies to what Poor Richard knew about digging wells. Fort Allen was garrisoned for five years. On its evacuation in January of 1761, the site on which it stood reverted to the Moravians,—being within the limits of a tract of 120 acres, part of a great tract of 5,000 acres released by William Penn to Adrian Vrœsen, of Rotterdam, in March of 1682, deeded by Adrian Vrœsen to Benjohan Furley, of the aforementioned city—surveyed for the heirs of Benjohan Furley, in December of 1735; conveyed in March of 1745, in its entirety, by Thomas Lawrence, of Philadelphia, attorney-at-law, for Dorothea, widow of Benjohan Furley, and Elizabeth and Martha Furley, coheirs of Benjohan Furley, to Edward Shippen, of Philadelphia, merchant; conveyed by Edward Shippen in September of 1745 to Richard Peters, of Philadelphia; Peters thereupon deeding the aforementioned 120 acres to Charles Brockden, of Philadelphia, for the use and behoof of the Moravians.

On the 23d of November, 1755, the house was for the first time occupied by the military, and in the evening of that day, Col. John Anderson of Greenwich, West Jersey, arrived with a detachment of sixty men, to aid a sister Province in distress. These passed the night at the Inn, and next day, taking the Gnadenhutten road (the same that had been laid out by order of the Court in 1748,—"a good wagon road from the King's Road near Bethlehem to the Mahoning creek"), set out for the mountain, where Indians painted for war were said to be lurking. Despite the presence of Anderson's men in the neighborhood, however, the savages, as is known, struck a blow that same evening at the Mahoning, which cost the Moravians eleven lives, and almost proved fatal to their prosperous mission.

Intelligence of this calamity moved Government to lose no more time in putting the exposed frontiers of Northampton in a posture of defence, and Franklin, hereupon, began to move companies of Bucks County militia to the scene of the recent disaster. Capt. Wilson, with sixty men, was the first to march. The company spent the night of the 26th and 27th of November at the Bethlehem Tavern, and then followed in the track of Anderson.

Franklin arrived at Bethlehem with Commissioners Fox and Hamilton on the 18th of December. With these came Capt. Trump's company of fifty men (their arms, ammunition and blankets, and a hogshead of rum for their use, writes Parsons, had been forwarded to Easton in advance), so that on the aforementioned day, one hundred and fifty souls, states a trusty chronicler, were billeted at our little Inn. This military triumviate now labored with alacrity, dividing the time until the expiration of the year between Easton and Bethlehem. They summoned Capts. Aston and Wayne from Bucks,—organized a new company at the former place in command of Capt. McLaughlin, and advised with Capts. Martin, Craig, and Hays of the Irish settlements in the Forks. "I had no difficulty," says Franklin in his autobiography, "in raising men, having soon five hundred and sixty under my command." From the 7th to the 15th of January, 1756, his headquarters were at Bethlehem. Having mustered into the service Capt. Volck's company, which arrived at the Inn from Allemaengel (Lynn township, Lehigh County) on the 11th of the aforementioned month, and commissioned John Nicholas Wetterhold in the Province pay, and John Van Etten of Upper Smithfield, Captains, — despite his modest confession that "he did not consider himself well qualified for the military business," — the Colonel set out for Gnadenhutten to erect a stockade at that important point.

It was the 15th of January, 1756, when he broke

camp at Bethlehem and moved his little army in the direction of the wilderness. He was surrounded by the pomp and circumstance of war — but we do not question for a moment that the sage's heart was in the chime of electrical bells, which was wont to ring musically in his quiet study, on High street, under the influence of that invisible agency, which he, first of men, drew down from the clouds.

Two days after his departure, Capt. Jacob Arndt, with fifty men, who had been ordered up from Rockland in Bucks, "to strengthen this part of the Province," so writes Franklin, "to convoy provisions to the company at work over the mountain, and to quiet the inhabitants who seem terrified out of their senses," halted at the Inn, and on the 18th of the last mentioned month, set out for their destination.*

On the 4th of February, Franklin returned to Bethlehem with an escort of thirty men. He had built his first fort. Kliest, the blacksmith, having shoed the Colonel's horse, for which the Province became indebted to the blacksmith in the sum of one and ninepence, and Lange, the saddler, having re-

*Jacob Arndt was an energetic and popular officer in the Indian wars, a leading patriot in the country of his adoption during the struggle for American Independence, and a member of the Supreme Executive Council of Pennsylvania. He died at Easton in 1805.

paired his saddle to the amount of three and six, the tired warrior,—his martial cloak still damp from the frosty rime of the mountain, if not wet with "the dew of battle,"—rode down to the ferry, was ferried across Lecha, and having watered his horse once more at the Inn, followed along the river's bank to the head of Ysselstein's Island, and there struck the great highway to the capital. This was on the fourth day of February, in the thirtieth year of his subjects' Sovereign Lord, King George the second, and in the year of our Lord, one thousand seven hundred and fifty-six.

It was Mr. Grabs' good fortune before retiring from the Inn, to witness, as we have just seen, the mustering of troops in defence of old Northampton, when she was, for the first time, invaded by Indians,—and, as landlord, to have added 17*l.* 12*s.* 3*d.*, to the revenue of his house during its military occupation. His last official act on record was the purchase of an hour-glass. Now, as a "Neisser clock," bearing the legend *Ab hoc momento pendet æternitas* was ticking in the narrow hall of the hostelry, ever since the days of Hartman Verdriess, we fail even to conjecture why so primitive a chronometer was added to the inventory of its effects. On the 9th of April of the last mentioned year, Mr. Grabs severed his connection with the Bethlehem Tavern.

It remains to be said of him, that in the ensuing summer he removed with his family to Bethabara, on the great Moravian tract, in Rowan County, North Carolina—that in July of 1759, he assisted in making a settlement at "Walnut Bottom," subsequently called Bethany, and that at Bethany he died in the spring of 1793.

Here it becomes incumbent upon us to retrace our footsteps in this excursion, in order to bring up the history of the important appendage to the hostelry, to whose fortunes those of the latter were closely linked. The Ferry was left, on a previous page, in the hands of Adam Schaus, whose return for the year ending 31st December, 1745, showed an income of only *2l. 11s. 2d.* (the rates in those days for a footman, were *3d.*, but for a horse and rider *6d.*)—a sum whose insignificance would surprise us, were we not advised, that in the absence of a grant and patent, it was thought prudent to make payment for ferriage altogether optional with travellers. Nevertheless, the advantages accruing to the Economy from a ferry at this point, were, it will be admitted, so decided as to almost outweigh even the consideration of gain.

On Schaus' appointment to the mill, one John David Behringer, shoemaker (he and Gertrude his wife, had immigrated in the autumn of 1743), who was domiciled in a log-house that stood just without the eastern line of the Simpson Tract* (it was long known as "the Behringer House," and appears to have partaken somewhat of the character of a penal institution), and Matthew Hoffman, born in Lischen† in Siegerland, in the Palatinate, but last from Oley in the County of Berks, saw-miller, consented to share the management and the responsibility of transportation over Lecha, until such time as an efficient ferryman should be found. Much to their chagrin, naturally enough, then, did a sudden rise in the wayward river (it was in the night of the 16th and 17th of February of 1747) tear the flat from her moorings, whence she was hurried

* *Dec. 6th,* 1745. David Behringer came to the house over against the saw-mill, November 16th, 1746. He is to be rent free one year, and pay 3*l.* per annum as long as he lives there, and to enjoy the customary privileges, excepting the fish-dam, and the rent of the farm." *Bethlehem Steward's Book.*—Mr. Behringer had occasional customers from points as remote as the Brodhead Settlement, or Dansbury on Analomink, in transmontane Bucks. "Dec. 3d, 1745, Daniel Brodhead, Dr. to J. D. Behringer, for mending shoes, 19*s.*" *Ibid.* We have failed to ascertain, when this historic house was built.

† If the curious reader would fix the locality of this and other towns and hamlets in the Palatinate named in the course of this narrative, he may consult that well-known and popular topographical manual, entitled "Historisch-geographischer Hand-Atlas zur Geschichte der Staaten Europas, vom Anfang des Mittelalters bis auf die neueste zeit, von Dr. Karl V. Spruner, Kœniglich Bayerischem Major und wirklichem Mitglied der Kœniglich Bayerischen Academie der Wissenschaften zu München. Gotha, bei Justus Perthes, 1854.

down the rapid stream and irretrievably lost. There was no alternative but to construct another. Now the second flat* that did service at the Bethlehem Ferry was launched on the 28th day of May, next following the above chronicled disaster, whereupon, Peter Petersen, last from Staten Island, mariner, was appointed her commander. During his admiralship, sometime in 1749, the first grant and patent for ferrying over the West Branch of Delaware, was procured from the Proprietaries' Secretary, at an annual rent of 5*s.*, by the Moravians at Bethlehem. This was done, we read, in order to meet the increasing uncertainty of remuneration resulting from a tacit appeal to the generosity of travellers, and also to secure themselves against a possibility of competition from some rival enterprise in the adjacent neutral waters of Lecha. It was now, too, that wharves were constructed at both termini for

* The following "memorandum for building a ferry-flat," without date and without signature, it is true, may possibly have been noted down for use at this time. "Length, 31½ feet. Breadth at the head, 7 feet 6 inches. Extreme breadth 9 feet. Abaft the head, 7 feet 8 inches. At the stern by a regular sweep from the extreme breadth, 7 feet 2 inches. Depth at the highest part of the side 24 inches. The shear 2 inches, to flare 3 inches. The sides to be sawed 5 inches thick at the bottom edge, and 3½ inches at the top edge. The head and stern posts 18 inches wide, and 8 inches thick on the front edge, and the bottom planks to rabbit on 5 inches—the bottom plank the whole length, and the cross plank the breadth of the flat; the whole 2 inches thick."

the more convenient ingress and egress of wagons, and the equipments of the ferry were completely renovated.

The spectrum presented to the view at this stage of our historical analysis, suddenly becomes a discontinuous one and is so crowded with absorption lines as to leave us in serious doubt as to the order in the succession of the different Charons, figuring in the scene. Nevertheless, a single luminous band, declares unmistakeably that Daniel Kunckler, a native of St. Gall, Canton St. Gall, Switzerland (he immigrated with Ann Mary, his wife, in the autumn of 1743 and settled at Nazareth), was ferryman in the year 1753.

When, in the spring of 1756, during the incumbency of the sixth landlord of the Inn, a second grant and patent (known in Moravian history as "the Great Ferry Patent") reconfirmed to the Moravian Society the sole privilege of ferrying across Lecha for the distance of one mile above and one mile below their settlement, and for a term of seven years, also,—a new impetus was given to the enterprise. A flat, forty-two feet in length was forthwith substituted for the one then in use,—and a "speaking-trumpet" (six shillings lawful money of Pennsylvania were paid to Abraham Hasselberg, the pewterer at Bethlehem, for the shell) added to the outfit. Now the following is a faithful copy of the instrument which conferred large privileges upon the holders of the ferry, and which, moreover, "dead-headed" the Honorable the Governor and his servants (its cost, including clerk's fees, was 1*l.* and 14*s.*), the original being endorsed,

Grant and Patent for the Bethlehem Ferry.

Thomas Penn and Richard Penn, Proprietaries, to David Nitschmann, of Bethlehem, carpenter, for seven years from March 2d, 1756.

Philadelphia, 10*th March,* 1756.

"**Whereas** it hath been represented to us, by reason of the late very considerable increase of settlements on both sides of the West Branch of the River Delaware and parts adjacent, and the great resort of people thither, and the many travelers whose business and affairs call them into those parts of the Province, and have occasion to pass over that branch of the said river, it is become necessary that some regular ferries at proper distances and places should be erected and established for the more ready and safe transporting all persons, cattle, carriages and goods over the said branch,—**And** it appearing to us upon the representation of David Nitschmann* of the County of Northampton in our

* David Nitschmann, the elder, a native of Moravia, and sprung from ancestors who were members of the ancient *Unitas Fratrum,* was the first Chief Proprietor of the estates of his Society in Pennsylvania; he

said Province, that the plantation belonging to the said David Nitschmann and company, and now in the occupation of the said David Nitschmann, situate in Saucon township in the said County of Northampton upon the highroad leading from the city of Philadelphia to the Minisinks, and from thence to the northwest parts of the Province of New York, by means of the convenient situation thereof on the sides of the said branch, is a suitable place for erecting and keeping a ferry over the same to Bethlehem in the Forks of Delaware, **And** the same David Nitschmann having requested our license for erecting and keeping a ferry there, and that we would grant and confirm the same to him, **Now know ye,** that in consideration of the charge and expenses which the said David Nitschmann must be put to in making wharves and landing-places and providing necessary flats and boats, and the constant attendance necessary thereunto, **And we** being always ready and willing to promote the public utility and improvement of our said Province, and to give due encouragement to all who shall undertake or contribute to the same, **Have** given, granted and confirmed, and by these Presents for us and our heirs **Do** give, grant and confirm unto the

having been qualified to assume them, in virtue of letters of denization granted him by the Provincial Court, in September of 1750. Prior to that date, the deeds for lands purchased by the Moravians were executed to individuals among them who were born subjects of the Crown of Great Britain. Nitschmann died at Bethlehem in April of 1758, and is popularly known as the founder of that place.

said David Nitschmann, his executors, administrators and assigns, the sole liberty and privilege of erecting, keeping and occupying a ferry over the said West Branch of the River Delaware to and from the place aforesaid for the transporting and carrying over the same all persons, wagons, carts and other carriages, horses, cattle, goods, wares, merchandises and things whatsoever, hereby strictly forbidding all other persons on either side of the said branch from taking or carrying over the same within the distance of one mile above and below the said ferry hereby settled and established, for hire, reward or pay, in any flat, boat or canoe, any persons, wagons, carts or other carriages, horses or cattle, **And** we do further give and grant unto the said David Nitschmann, his executors, administrators and assigns during the term hereby demised, the liberty and privilege to demand and receive from all persons, and for all wagons, carts and other carriages, horses and other cattle, goods, wares, merchandises, and things whatsoever passing or being carried over the said ferry all such reasonable toll, fees, or reward as shall be settled for the same (us our heirs and successors and our Lieutenant Governor and attendants and servants only excepted), **To have and to hold** the said ferry, liberties, privileges, profits and advantages hereby granted, with the appurtenances, unto the said David Nitschmann, his executors, administrators and assigns,—from the second day of March instant for and during and unto the full end and term of seven years thence next ensuing fully to be complete and ended, *Yielding and paying* therefor yearly to us our heirs and successors at the town of Easton in the said County of Northampton on every the first day of March in every year for and during the said term hereby granted five English silver shillings or value thereof in coin current according as the exchange shall be between our said Province and the city of London, to such person or persons as shall from time to time be appointed to receive the same, *Provided* always that if the same David Nitschmann, his executors, administrators or assigns shall not at all times during the said term hereby granted, find, provide and maintain necessary and sufficient flats and boats for the use of the said ferry, and give due, constant and ready attendance thereunto, that then and from thenceforth this present grant shall cease, determine and be void, anything herein before mentioned and contained to the contrary thereof in any wise notwithstanding."

Whoever has made the great wave of Palatine immigration which rolled across the Atlantic in the first half of the eighteenth century, a special study, will recall the fortunes of those three thousand and more Germans, whom Queen Anne's most excellent Majesty, "out of her unlimited compassion and constant goodness," caused to be transported to the new world in the Lyon of Leith, the Herbert frigate, the Berkley Castle and divers other ships of burden,—how, on landing at New York in June of 1710, the Mayor of that city, having just cause to believe that there were many contagious distempers among them, consigned them to quarantine on Nutten (now Governor's Island)—how, in the ensuing autumn, they were settled on both shores of Hudson's river; on the east shore in Dutchess County along Roeloff Jansen's kill in the villages of Hunterstown, Queensbury and Annesbury; but on the west shore in Albany county along Sawyer's kill, in Elisabethtown and Georgetown, — how, they were expected to engage in the production of rosin, pitch, tar and turpentine for the use of the British navy (the overplus, however, to be turned to a beneficial trade with Spain and Portugal), they having been promised sustenance until such time as they could reap the benefit of their labor, — how, in 1713, finding it impossible to make tar where there were no pines, they began to remove to Scoharie, for which her Grace, the Queen, had contracted with the Indians in their behalf prior to the immigration,—how they were hospitably received there by the Mohawk sachems, — how Governor Hunter thereupon covertly sold Scoharie to land-jobbers in Albany—and how after years of contest with these gentlemen's agents and of struggling with poverty, the brave Palatines, gathering together their wives and children, their flocks and their herds, boldly cut a way through the wilderness to the head waters of the Susquehanna, built them canoes, and while the old men paddled the women and children down the courses of that marvellously beautiful river to the mouth of the fretful Swatara, the sturdier yeomen drove the oxen, the horses, the sheep and the swine overland through a trackless forest, until (it was in the summer of 1733) they reached their destination in the pastoral valley of the Tulpehocken, where they set up their household gods, and founded a German state in the very heart of the Indian country, and beyond the jurisdiction of the British lion, much to the dissatisfaction, be it said, of that magnanimous king.

John Frederic Schaeffer, the seventh landlord of our Inn, was a son of one of these adventurous Palatines, to wit; the oldest son of Michael Schaeffer, and Elisabeth his wife, and was born in Scoharie, in March of 1722. He was therefore a boy at the time of his people's exodus.

From Tulpehocken (where the Moravians had a firm foothold until in 1747, when by reason of "a wrong direction having been given by rivals to the tenor of a deed" executed to them by the Proprietaries for the confirmation of a parcel of land in their manor of Plumpton, they lost it) young Schaeffer removed to Bethlehem, where, in December of 1746, he married Jannetje, relict of Philip Rudolph Haymer of Saucon township, but oldest daughter of Isaac Martens Ysselstein, last from Marbletown in Esopus, and Rachel, née Bogart, his wife. He was settled at Gradenthal on the Barony, at the time of his appointment to the Inn, over whose fortunes he presided from the 9th of April, to the 18th of October, 1756.

This interval though brief, proved an eventful period in its history. The last of the refugees who had found an asylum under its hospitable roof after the irruption of the savages into cis-montane Northampton on New Year's day, had returned to their homes; the echoes of martial sounds had died away—the old *habitués* of the house again frequented their accustomed haunts—and there began to brood a spirit of listless repose over the precincts of the hostelry as in the palmy days of Jobst Vollert and Hartmann Verdries. Meanwhile Government had taken a step which conjured up the storm that demonstrated this calm to have been an ominous lull, and which brought a swarm of hungry locusts from the wilderness to sorely plague John Nicholas Schaeffer, and after his retirement from public life, Ephraim Culver, the eighth landlord of the Bethlehem Inn. In the face of a formal declaration of war, Governor Morris was led in June of 1756 to proffer the olive branch to the disaffected Indians. Accordingly he dispatched messengers to the enemy's headquarters at Tioga with an invitation for their chief men and counsellers to come down and meet him in conference. This invitation met with a response,—thus opening a new epoch in the history of our Inn—which may, not improperly, be styled the epoch of Indian occupation. Full seventeen months elapsed before it closed.*

The appearance at the Bethlehem Tavern on the 17th day of July of the last mentioned memorable year of "a lusty, raw-boned man, haughty and very desirous of respect and command," a Delaware of the Unamis, "dressed in a fine dark-brown cloth coat laced with gold, which had been given him recently by the French at Niagara, caused a profound sensation among the inmates of the hostelry. They recognized an old acquaintance—Gideon of the Gnadenhutten Mission—in a new character as Tadeuskundt, the Delaware King. "This is the man," writes Parsons, "who persuaded his people to go over to the French and then to attack our frontiers." The chieftain was attended by a wild company of adherents, men, women and children—(thirty-one all told), the women wearing shirts, as was observed, "made of Dutch table cloths," some of the *spolia*

* For full particulars of what occurred at the Bethlehem Tavern during this occupation, we would point the reader to "The Account of the United Brethren at Bethlehem with the Commissioners of the Province of Pennsylvania, during the Indian War of 1755, '56, and '57," in the first Volume of the *Memorials of the Moravian Church. Phila., J. B. Lippincott & Co.* 1870.

opima taken in the last winter's forays into upper Northampton.

These unwelcome guests Mr. Schaeffer had orders from the Commissioners to entertain;—in fact, the orders of that body to him and his successors in office provided for the entertainment at the Bethlehem Inn (until the restoration of peace), of all Indians coming that way who had or who might have business with Government. Now for the King and his great men our worthy landlord provided until their departure for Easton, and for several days on their return from a treaty, which had formally opened at that place on the 28th of July, between Governor Morris, on the part of the Province, and Tadeuskundt on the part of the Delawares. So it came to pass that the King ran up a score of 1*l.* 17*s.* at Schaeffer's, for eating and drinking (to the latter he was much addicted, Parsons stating that "he could consume three quarts or a gallon of rum a day without becoming drunk")—the King's oldest son, a score of 10*l.* 14*s.* 2*d.* for sundries, and Elisabeth, the Queen, one of 5*l.* 19*s.* 2*d.* "for victualing herself and three children from the 21st August to the 1st of October, being forty-one days, at two and six pence per day."

In the next place, the Governor having ordered Conrad Weisser (the rank of Colonel had been conferred upon the veteran interpreter in October of

1755, for meritorious conduct at Tolheo) to come up from Heidelberg, in Berks, with whatever troops could be spared, it being his opinion "that it was quite necessary to have a good number of soldiers at Easton during the sessions of the conference,"—the Colonel and his men sojourned at our Inn both on their way to and on their return from that place. Thereupon Mr. Schaeffer preferred the following charges against them, to wit:

		l.	s.	d.
July 27, 1756.	"For supper and breakfast for 48 men, Conrad Weisser and company, including hay for ye horses, ...	3	1	
Aug. 1,	On their return from Easton for dinner to the same company, ...	1	17	6
		4	18	6

Besides entertaining these celebrities, and soldiers sent from Fort Allen on detached service (there was scarcely a week but what some corporal's squad would halt at the Inn, and in July Lieut. McAlpine and Ensign Jeffry of the Royal Americans opened a recruiting office in the house), Mr. Schaeffer was providing for several families of friendly Indians, who had passed the enemy's lines, and since June had been quartered upon him by order of Government. In this way his time and attention were fully engaged for the remaining months of his incumbency, during which, it is on record, the Province of Pennsylvania became indebted to the Bethlehem Tavern in the sum of fifty pounds currency.*

A New Englander by birth and education was the eighth in the succession of landlords at our Inn. This was Ephraim Culver—a native of the town of Lebanon, Litchfield County, Connecticut — who, sharing with his countrymen their innate propensity to migrate, had exchanged the land of steady habits for the wilds of Smithfield, in upper Northampton, whence he fled to the Barony on the irruption of the savages in December of 1755. At Nazareth he united with the Moravians, to whom he had been previously attached. Although a miller, his appointment to the Inn was in all respects a happy one as the sequel proved. In fact, as we shall see, he spent fourteen consecutive years of his life in the capacity of landlord at Moravian Inns; and further testimonial to his eminent fitness for so responsible a position, would be supererogatory. None of these years, however, were as momentous or as full of incident as were the first two of his incumbency at the Bethle-

*John Nicholas Schaeffer died at Nazareth in April of 1807. Frederic, a son, died at the same place in June of 1830, and Elizabeth, a granddaughter, at Bethlehem, in July of 1857.

hem Tavern, which incumbency we shall proceed to review as briefly as is consistent with the just proportions of this history.

A second conference with the "enemy Indians" convened at Easton on the 8th day of November next after Mr. Culver's entrance upon public life. This brought grist to his new mill at once. The Delawares must needs pass and repass by Bethlehem. There was a charm for them in its environs. And so it happened that in the evening of the 17th of the aforementioned month Mr. Culver and Elisabeth, m. n. Smith, from "The Oblong" in Dutchess County, New York, his wife, were called upon at short notice to provide a hot supper for forty-one Indians (the treaty had closed that afternoon), and at the same time to furnish them with forty-six quarts of beer, and then hay for their fourteen horses. But King Tadeuskundt called for two quarts of wine for himself and his counsellor Tapescohung, and for two quarts of oats for his beast. Next morning at their departure this merry company was supplied with one hundred and ten pounds of bread and two gallons of cider.

The following memorandum extracted from the waste-book of the clerk of the Inn introduces us to some of the soldiers, whose presence at Easton it was intended should lend solemnity to the conference, and impress the Indians effectually with the military resources of the Province.

	l.	s.	d.
"Nov. 17, 1756. Capt. Runals and Lieutenant Wetherhold Counrod Wiser soldier one Insign one Drummer which came with the Indians from the Treety, Dr. for Supper and 1 pint wine, . .		3	6
Seven quarts beer, 1 dram, . .		2	8
Five horses hay and oats and these mens Lodging, ...		5	10
The Soldier with an express from the Governor from Easton to Redden for eating and drinking and horse keeping on hay and oats, . .		5	2
		17	2"

Old Tatamy (Tot's Gap* in the Blue Mountain bears the chieftain's name to the present day) ate at the Inn on the day after the treaty; and Sam Evans and Young Capt. Harris, half-brothers to the King, were inmates of the house to the close of the month. It should have been stated that Governor Denny rode over to Bethlehem in the evening of the 17th of November, spent the night in the town,† and the

*On following the "Tot's Gap Road," as you leave Rocksbury, in Upper Mount Bethel, you come to this pass over the Mountain, four short miles west from the Delaware Water Gap.

†It may interest some local antiquarian to know that in the absence of a public house at Bethlehem, at this time, a set of apartments on the second floor of the old stone house on Market street, built in 1753 for a store, were kept furnished for the accommodation of visitors of note. As Franklin, among others, lodged here occasionally during his cam-

following morning set out for Philadelphia. He was the first Lieutenant Governor who enjoyed the immunity provided for his rank and station by the thoughtful Proprietaries in their Great Patent for the Bethlehem Ferry.

Passing over incidents of minor importance which crowded the first months of the year 1757, at our Inn — to wit: the preparations made by Jo Peepy and Lewis Montour, when on the eve of a mission in behalf of the Province to Tioga — the death of John Smalling, a grandson of the King, who died of small-pox and was buried in the cemetery on the Simpson Tract, for ten shillings — the maintenance of fifty-nine Indians who loitered about the house since the close of the treaty — the maintenance of such as were constantly on the wing between Fort Allen and Easton, or Fort Allen and Philadelphia — Hugh Crawford's two days' sojourn — and the presence of sundry lieutenants and ensigns at sundry times — we come to the month of July, in the last week of which month a third meeting for a treaty with the Indians opened at Easton. This was an important conference, and as its deliberations were expected to be on grave subjects, and touching the confirmation of peace, too, it was more numerously attended than

paign on the frontiers, the house is justly entitled to more than ordinary historical distinction, and to the name of "The Franklin House."

either of the preceding. A motley crowd of savages at the Bethlehem Tavern a week before the appointed day, heralded its approach, and on the 8th of August, (the very day of its close) seventy-five of the barbarians supped at Culver's — and then called each for a half gill of rum and a pint of cider. From the tenth to the fifteenth of the month there were daily one hundred and fifty at table, and when not at table, at large on the premises. But these had things their own way. This is inferable from complaints lodged against them with the Commissioners by the people at the Inn, to the effect that the Indians engaged in robbing orchards and gardens on the Simpson Tract, that they wrangled over their cups, and that they occasionally visited Bethlehem, where they would vary their excesses, by discharging their fire-arms at random and breaking lights in the windows. The King it is true, was present; so was Paxanosa, a king of the Shawanose. But neither their joint majesties, nor the high standing in Indian society of French Margaret, a niece of old Madam Montour of Otzinachson, or West Branch of Susquehanna, could restrain this lawless crew from holding carnival as it chose. The King meanwhile ran up a score of 10*l.* 18*s.* 9*d.*, Paxanosa bought him a pair of spectacles, with which he paraded the streets of Bethlehem to the wonderment of its little boys — while French Margaret, with the fondness for colors instinctive in her sex, although she had passed the grand climacteric, invested in two pounds of vermilion. It was now that Indian occupation of the Bethlehem Inn had reached its zenith. Hereafter it waned.

In the evening of the 7th of August, Gov. Denny arrived at Bethlehem. Declining an invitation to lodge in the town, he crossed the ferry, and passed the night at Culver's. Here he was serenaded by the musical element of the town from boats on the river. In what manner he acknowledged the compliment, and whether, betwixt flute, viol and bassoon, and seventy-five Indians, he suffered from insomnia or not,—the annalist has failed to record.

Three days after his Honor's departure, William Tatamy—son of old Tatamy who died at the house of John Jones* in Bethlehem township from the

* John Jones was born in 1714, in Upper Merion, then in Philadelphia county. His father had immigrated from Wales with "other persons of excellent and worthy character, descendants of the ancient Britons," principally from Radnor, Brin-Maur and Haverford, in Merionethshire. Through their itinerants, Jones became acquainted with the Moravians, and was induced in 1749 to locate with his young family in the vicinity of Bethlehem, where he followed his trade, that of a blacksmith. In April of 1751, he purchased of Patrick Graeme, of Philadelphia (a brother of Dr. Thomas Graeme, and one of the proprietors of Bachelor's Hall, "a place of gluttony and good living," on its outskirts), a desirable tract of 500 acres of land on the left bank of the Lehigh and touching the east line of the Moravian lands. John Jones, the ancestor of the Joneses, of Bethlehem township, died on his farm, in June of 1781, but

effects of a gunshot wound he had received at the hands of a reckless boy in the Craig settlement, while on his way to Easton with Tadeuskundt's Indians, (this was on the 7th of July)—was buried in the grave-yard hard by the Inn, also, on the same day a Delaware woman from Lechawachneck (Pittston), one of the King's company.

For some weeks after his subjects' return to the Susquehanna, Tadeuskundt divided his time between Fort Allen and Philadelphia. Having arranged with Government for the building of a town for himself and his people in Wyoming Valley on the opening of spring, and having purchased of one James Burd, merchant in the aforementioned city, a regimental coat and a gold-laced hat and cockade—the old man returned to Bethlehem. Here he passed the winter in a cabin which the Moravians built for him near their Inn* with the approval of the Provincial Com-

---

was buried in the grave-yard at Bethlehem. His children were educated at Moravian schools. Jesse, a son, was collector of excise for Northampton County prior to the Revolution. The house in which young Tatamy was nursed stood on the site of the late residence of George Jones.

* Reuter's valuable draft of "Moravian lands lying on the south side of the Lehigh," drawn in 1757 (this draft is referred to more fully on a later page), designates three cabins located on said draft on the river's bank, in front of the building at present occupied by the offices of the Lehigh Valley Railroad Company,—"Indians." Here then dwelt that troublesome people, which the government saw fit to impose upon the Moravians during the Indian War. Perhaps the King's winter-house was blocked up on this same plot.

missioners. But he and his family until their departure for the Indian Country, drew daily rations from the Bethlehem Tavern. The income of the house during the busy period which we have just reviewed, was, as we might expect, unusually large. Its net profits for the year ending 31st December, 1757, amounted to 195*l.* 10*s.* 11*d.* We believe they were never exceeded in any twelve months subsequently.

George Klein, from Kirchart, in the Lower Palatinate (he had immigrated to the Province in 1727, and settled in Conestoga, where he married Ann Bender), is entitled, perhaps, to rank among the landlords of the Inn, in as far as he relieved Mr. Culver on one occasion for several months during the latter's incumbency. This is the same Klein who donated some two hundred and fifty acres of land to the Moravians (they had been deeded to Klein by one Jacob Baer, in 1737) for a settlement,—which since 1762, has developed into the unique village of Litiz, in Warwick township, Lancaster County. But the "Klein Tract is watered by Carter's Run, which heads in a spring remarkable at once for the volume of water it throws out, and for exhibiting a natural phenomenon rarely seen,—it having been observed that as often as a leaf falls tremblingly from the overhanging aspens,—up from the transparent depths of the fountain there rises a second trembling like unto its fellow, until the twin shapes mingle upon the surface of the pellucid pool. This *fons sacer* is known as "The Great Spring," or "The Litiz Spring," and yet some profanely, forsooth, care it "Venus' Mirror."

King Tadeuskundt bade adieu to Bethlehem on the 16th of May, 1758, much to the relief of Mr. Culver, whose last year at the Inn consequently proved to be one of comparative repose. Having accepted an appointment to "The Rose" on the Barony of Nazareth, our well-tried host set out for that place in March of 1759. We shall meet him again before the close of this narrative.

Andrew Horne and Dorothea, his wife, who immigrated in the autumn of 1744, directed the affairs of the Bethlehem Tavern during the next triennium. A reference to the docket kept by the clerk of the Court of General Quarter Sessions for the County of Northampton shows that Mr. Horne was twice recommended to his Honor, the Governor, as "a fit person to keep a house of entertainment in said County." This administration was not an eventful one. Its close, however (Mr. Horne retired in March of 1762), marks an important change in the polity of the Moravians in Pennsylvania, which change, after the loose threads of this history, shall have been woven rightly into its web up to the date of its inauguration, shall be duly considered.

To do the former, we must here turn back in order to follow the improvements which had been progressing on the Simpson Tract since the erection of a barn in 1747, and to notice the condition of the Bethlehem Ferry. In February of 1752, water was led in pipes from a spring in the mountain side, just without the south line of the tract, so as to irrigate the lowlands and increase the border of natural meadow, that skirted the run, which, in the rainy season, poured tribute into the Lecha, debouching into the ravine east of the Inn.* A draft of "Beth-

*Some readers of these pages may remember that thirty years ago, decaying fruit trees and the foundation walls of a dwelling in ruins, were to be seen on the ascent of the mountain, at a spot now included within the grounds of the Lehigh University. The spot was for years a favorite resort for such of the people of Bethlehem as loved to recreate themselves with cake and coffee under green trees and by running water in pleasant summer afternoons, and was familiarly called "The Old Man's Place." Its origin, for want of a history, was naturally enough involved in tradition, and next in fable and mystery. It was said to have been the retreat of an anchorite—of an alchemist in search of the philosopher's stone and the elixir vitæ. Now these remains were the relics of a three-acre improvement made by old John Lischer, of Oley, in 1750, on a tract of 87 acres, which the Moravians purchased of the Honorable Proprietaries two years later, whereupon Lischer sold out his claim for 9*l.*, and removed elsewhere. "The Old Man's Place" or "The Hermitage" (so it is called in the Journal kept by the misses of the Boarding School in 1788, in which year, that journal states, there were on the spot the "ruins of an old cabin and twelve apple trees"), was included in the 115 acres of woodland which Asa Packer purchased of the Moravians in 1853.

lehem Lands on the South of the Lecha," drawn by C. G. Reuter in July of 1757 (Mr. Reuter immigrated in 1756, removed to North Carolina in 1759, where he was actively engaged until his decease at Salem in 1777, as surveyor and draftsman)—shows the following to have been the condition of the Tract in that year. The one hundred and ten acres on the west side of the Salisbury road were unbroken woodland and heavily timbered; east of that road, and as far as the run (this was lined at intervals by meadow, amounting in all to eight acres), down to the river, we find thirty-seven acres under cultivation, a stretch of forty acres on the river's bank extending from the run to the east line of the tract also under the plow, and seventy-nine acres of woodland, stretching south of the same up the first acclivity of the mountain. Reuter's draft furthermore, shows a large barn two hundred and forty feet due east from the Inn, which was in course of erection in the summer of 1757. There was no material change of this status (saving some small clearings) until subsequent to the dissolution of the Bethlehem Economy in 1762.

We left the Bethlehem Ferry in the hands of Daniel Kunckler. Now its growing prosperity under Proprietary patronage suggesting a change in its construction, in January of 1758, it was converted into a rope-ferry, being ever afterwards conducted on the mysterious principles of the parallelogram of forces, which such form of ferry involves. A chronicler of that day in noting this improvement, observes with somewhat of enthusiasm, that "whereas, formerly in times of high water four men found it difficult to effect a passage in less than half an hour, the flat crosses the river by the rope usually in ninety seconds." Time, therefore, was made, and time even then was money. John Garrison, a son of Capt. Nicholas Garrison of the Irene (whose name is being gratefully perpetuated by one of the streets of the borough of Bethlehem), was appointed ferryman in September of 1758, Daniel Kunckler, a second time in 1759, and Francis Steup, in October of 1761. The following entry in the Economy's Ledger, under date of November 9th, 1761, indicates that improvements in the important appendage to the Bethlehem Inn, had not ceased;—"Paid for ninety fathoms of shroud hawser, pulleys and tackling for the ferry-flat 22*l.* 18*s.* 2½*d.*"

Before pursuing this history into the new period which dawned upon the Bethlehem Inn and all things else on the Simpson Tract, in the spring of 1762, it remains for us to enumerate the worthies residing in the neighborhood of Bethlehem, who, when on business or in search of relaxation, availed themselves of its proffered hospitality, during the seventeen years which we have just reviewed. These, and not occasional wayfarers, it should be borne in mind, gave life and character to the house, stamping it with their individuality, regulating its intellectual commodities, and by the expression of their views on the weather, the crops, the politics and the news of the day, investing it in the natural order of things with all the importance of a rural exchange. Now Saucon township, as we may expect, furnished most of the knights who thus tilted at joust or tournament under the roof of the old Bethlehem Inn.—Thence came Joerg Freyman, Philip Kratzer, Hans Fahs, Michael Weber, Friedrich Weber, Peter Graff, miller, Balzar Beil, Balzar Lahr, Christian Laubach, miller on Laubach's Creek (he died in 1768), Friedrich Laubach, Anton Lerch (*altvater*, died in 1793), Peter Lerch, Kratzer Lerch, Johann Jacob Gross, Joerg Peter Knecht, Hans Landis, Dieter Gauff, Joerg Raub, Joerg Bachmann (whose orchard furnished cider for the Bethlehem Inn, during the first decade of its existence), Rudolph Oberly, Jacob Gangwehr, Matthias Riegel (*altvater*), Heinrich Groessman, Richard Freeman (the ancestor of the Freemans of Freemansburg, born in 1717 in Cecil County, Maryland, died in 1784, and buried on his farm called the "Private Heck"), Christian Heller, Ludwig Heller, Stoffel Heller, Simon Heller (the latter we believe is the same who settled near Wind Gap, and yet the genealogies of the Hellers, for a want of visitations of the heralds, are perplexing), Richard Ley, Valentine Santee, Anthony Boehm (a son of Rev. John Philip Boehm of Whitpaine township, Philadelphia County, to whom there were patented by the three Penns, in 1740, two hundred acres of land situate on the Saucon Creek, which tract he and his wife Ann Mary, "for and in consideration of the natural love and affection which they have and do bear for and toward their son" deeded to the aforesaid Anthony in September of 1747), besides Boyers, Ruchs, Transous, Reidenauers, Hesses and Weitknechts.

From Macungy and Salisbury there would come to the Bethlehem Inn, with produce for the Bethlehem market, Bastian Knauss, Jacob Ehrenhardt, Martin Bomberger, Heinrich Guth (sometime a disciple of Conrad Beissel), Jean Ditter *alias* Piper, Jean Ditter the younger (whose account in the Economy's Ledger is debited with two jackets and a pair of jumps* with whalebone, for his daughter Marguerite),

* An eminent lexicographer tells us that *jumps* were "a kind of limber stays or waistcoat worn by females;" and an equally eminent etymologist assures us that the word is derivable from Fr. *jupe*, a long petticoat, Pr. *jupa*, L. Lat. *jupa*, *juppa*, It. *giubba*, *giuppa*, Sp. *al-juba* from Ar. *al-jubbah*. Hence it would be erroneous to confound the article of apparel purchased by her fond father for his Marguerite, with another of feminine full dress, much in vogue in our own day, of which the name *jumps*, might be suggestive to the mind of some incautious reader.

Casper Kræmer *alias* "Der lange Kasper," Martin Gingineger, Friedrich Kemmerer, Nicolaus Gemperling (who stands charged to this day ten shillings for "curing his leg which was broken" in May of 1746), Adam Blanck, Adam Stocker, Heinrich Ritter, Franz Roth, Rudolph Schmidt, David Giesy, Michael Schweyer, Conrad Wetzel and Jacob Zimmermann.

But the Cruikshank farm sent Quash and Andrew (slaves from Montserrat), and the Jennings farm, old Solomon, and John and Isaiah his sons. From Forks Ferry came Adam Merckel, Christian Minier, Heinrich Hertzel, Conrad Bittenbender, Michael Moore and David English the ferryman; — from the Menagassi, old Peter Schuelpp with famous butter;—from "The Drylands," Valentine Kraeter, Michael Koch, Michael Klaus, Eberhardt Kreiling and Jacob Abel (some of whom in September of 1752, were convicted "as disturbers of the peace of our Lord the King for having unlawfully entered into and taken possession of land included within the Proprietaries' Manor of Fermor, neither located nor surveyed by any warrant or order from said Proprietaries,—and who thereupon were arrested and to the gaol of our Lord the King in the County of Bucks, were caused to be led");—from the adjacents of Nazareth, north, Philip Bossert, Franz Clevel and George Clevel;—from the adjacents of Nazareth, east, Abraham Lefevre and Johannes Lefevre;—from the adjacents of Nazareth, west, Simon Tromm, Philip Tromm, Friedrich Scholl, Peter Doll, Hannickel Heil and Friedrich Althomus;—from the Craig Settlement of Ulster Scots on heads of Calisuck and Menagassi, on market days with flax of their wives' spinning the following; to wit: Hugh Wilson (from Cootehill, County Cavan, Ulster), James Horner, Thomas Craig, William Craig, James Craige, Robert Gregg, Robert Dobbin, Samuel Brown, Robert Clendinen, James Carruthers, Robert Alison, John McCartney, Samuel Barron, John Redhill, James Gray, John Boyd, James Kerr, John McNair, William McCaa, James Ralston, Thomas Heron, Archibald Barron, Robert Lattimore, Robert Gibson, John McLean, Archibald Greer, Patrick McCullough, Giles Windsor, Thomas Thompson, Patrick Sufferan, John Campbell, Rowland Smith, Patrick Evans, James McLeary, Daniel Burr, James Eggleston and Joseph Perry;—from the Minisinks with deer skins and horns for barter, Daniel Brodhead, Adam (his slave), Daniel Roberts, Hermanus Decker, Joseph Haines, Francis Jones, Samuel Vanarmen, John Aguder and John George Salade;—and statedly, iron men from Durham, from Hopewell, Chelsea and Greenwich Forges, from Popadickon, and from Oxford Furnace and the Union Iron Works, in quest of Moravian manufactures, or the Moravian

Doctor's services, in return for bar-iron and stove plates.*

Thus the Bethlehem Inn was peopled by men of diverse nationalities in the days of the olden time; for the fame of the goodly house had gone abroad.

It was indeed a great change which the dissolution of the Economy at Bethlehem, in the spring of 1762, brought with it for the Moravians in Pennsylvania. For twenty years its members had been associated almost as closely as the members

---

*Bethlehem 4th May, 1746. Marcus Hulings of Durham, Dr.

	l.	s.	d.
To curing the bellows-maker's leg that was broken,	3	0	0
" " the man that hurt his ribs, ...	0	3	0
" bleeding himself, ...	0	1	0
" " one of his miners, ...	0	1	0
	3	5	0

JOHN MATTHEW OTTO, M. D.

Greenwich Iron Works, 12 July, 1750.

MR. FREDERIC OERTER, Clerk at Bethlehem,

Sir:

This is to desire you to please to order something from Doctor Otto to cure persons that is poisoned in mowing grass—and please order your saddler to make conveniences in my saddle to carry a pistol on each side. I have been informed that you have a set of wagon wheels ready made. If you have, I should be glad if you would send them along with your wagon, and you will much oblige

Your humble servant,

JACOB STARN.

P. S. Pray don't fail to send above things when your wagon next comes this way for iron.

of a family, actuated like the latter by a common interest and pursuing a common purpose. In view of their circumstances in those early times, this form of social constitution was, without doubt, wisely adopted by them for the attainment of the object for which they had removed to the new world. Under its influence they hoped to be able to concentrate their powers for the vigorous prosecution of that object, which was a mission among the aboriginies. This, however, had received a severe blow in the Indian war;—directly, in as far as its organization was almost irreparably deranged—and indirectly, in consequence of a change in the relations hitherto existing between the whites and their copper-colored neighbors. Nor could their own members fail to perceive tokens of a decay in their polity, such as eventually manifests itself in all states founded upon principles which unduly disregard the interest and claims of the individual with too high a regard for those of the commonwealth. These considerations moved Count Zinzendorf, who controlled the affairs of the Moravian Church until his death in 1760, to urge the dissolution of the Bethlehem Economy at as early a day as was consistent with a just provision for the welfare of those by whose labors it had been so long sustained. This dissolution was finally effected in April of 1762. It involved an entire reconstruction of the relation of labor in the little community, the members of which hereafter followed occupations for their own emolument, or conducted branches of industry for the Proprietor of the estates at a fixed compensation. In this way it came to pass that the Bethlehem Inn, in April of the last mentioned year was intrusted to a salaried agent, and that, with all things else which it had, forever passed from under a patriarchal form of government, it changed its mask to play a different role. Elated now at its new character, or jealous, perhaps, of a rival claimant for popular favor on the other side (the Sun Inn, which after a lingering struggle into existence had been completed so far as to entertain "guests" for the first time on the 25th of September, 1760),—our house clamored for a distinctive name. Hereupon the Moravians, who were a loyal people, having been the recipients of numerous favors at the hands of the British Crown, named it DAS GASTHAUS ZUR KRONE,—DIE KRONE,—THE CROWN,—and emblazoned that ancient emblem of royalty upon a sign-board which swung on a post near the head of the lane leading from the highway to its hospitable portal.*

* That rare, and by the antiquary highly prized, view of Bethlehem in the latter days of the Economy, drawn by Nicholas Garrison, Jr., and engraved on copper by J. Noual (it was published November 24th, 1757),

John Lischer, a native of Hilzoff, margraviate of Wittgenstein, in the Palatinate, but last from Oley, Berks County, was the first landlord of The Crown, he and his wife Catharine, née Loesch, from Tulpehocken, having been installed in office on the 27th day of March, 1762. They stipulated to administer the affairs of the Inn in consideration of their living, and 25*l.* Pennsylvania currency per annum,—and their hostler to assume the duties incumbent upon him for 10*l.* and the customary perquisite of *Trinkgeld.* Now the house, together with its appurtenances, was on the aforementioned day appraised at 267*l.* 19*s.*

Mr. Lischer, after having replenished his chambers, his kitchen and larder (we find that in the charming month of June, he added the luxury of napkins to his table service), and having acted upon the suggestion of his employers to raise poultry largely—"provided their presence do not conflict with the interests of the farm"—engaged also in apiculture, erecting an elaborate apiary or bee-house which in time yielded luscious comb for the hungry traveller. From one George Schlosser of Philadel-

shows the Inn in the foreground, and a sign-post with swinging board, near the head of the lane. From this it would appear that the hostelry then already bore a device as well as a name. These may have been "The Crown," but that appellation does not appear in official records until in 1762, as stated above.

phia, grocer, he purchased his needed supplies of Antigua, Barbadoes and New England rums, Lisbon and Madeira, coffee, sugar and limes, and favorite brands of roll-tobacco, known in those days specifically as "pig-tail," "hog-tail," and "cut-and-try." But neighbor Jones levied upon all things spirituous at the Inn for excise, mulcting it on the 29th of June, 1762, in the sum of 3*l.* 9*s.* 4*d.* for two hundred and forty-four gallons of liquor in store. The Christian's Spring Economy supplied The Crown with small beer, Christian Diemer, the baker at Bethlehem with bread, and Henry G. Krause, the butcher, with beef;—the latter staple commodity being delivered over ye water into the hands of Mistress Lischer at the rate of three pence per pound. In this way all honorable steps were taken to place the hostelry upon a sound working basis; its head had grown to be popular, and the routine of its daily life* was differing none from that of other rural Inns as the weeks and months passed by, when in the summer of 1763, there came rumors of Indian incursions in the then far West, and of

*At this time, new names appear in the records of the Inn—to wit: those of John Sevitz, Jonas Weber, Henry Brunner, Tobias Wendel, George Edelman, Henry Geisinger and William Stuber, inhabitants of the two Saucons; John Jæger, from the Drylands Berndt Straub, Mattes Schœner, Ludwig Frantz, Andrew Raub, Benjamin Riegel, Johannes Gœtz, and Hannes Melchior.

an impending Indian war. At the very time when the Ottawa chieftain Pontiac was prosecuting the siege of Detroit (12th May to 12th October), in the course of that mighty effort to drive the English from the country, for which he had enlisted all the western tribes,—lesser war-parties, at the bidding of their great leader, had crossed the Alleghanies and were committing depredations upon the frontiers of the Province. Before daybreak on the morning of the 8th of October, some Delaware warriors attacked the house of John Stenton, in Allen township (Stenton's house is remembered by aged residents of Weaversville as standing on the main road from Bethlehem to Mauch Chunk, eight miles northwest from the former place, on the property owned by the widow of the late Thomas Fatzinger), knowing that Capt. Jacob Wetterhold of the Province service with a squad of men was lodging there for the night. Meeting with Jean the wife of James Horner, who was on her way to a neighbors for coals to light her morning's fire, the Indians, fearing that she might betray them or raise an alarm, despatched her with their tomahawks.* Thereupon they surrounded Stenton's. No sooner had Capt.

---

* You may read her obituary record in the cemetery of the English Presbyterian Church of Allen Township, in these words:

"In memory of Jean, the wife of James Horner, who suffered death at the hands of savage Indians, 8th October, 1763, aged 50 years."

Wetterholds' servant stepped out of the house (he had been sent to saddle the Captain's horse) than he was shot down. The report brought his master to the door, when on opening it he received a mortal wound. Sergeant Lawrence McGuire, in his attempt to draw him in, was also dangerously wounded and fell. Thereupon the Lieutenant advanced. He was confronted by an Indian, who, leaping upon the bodies of the fallen men, presented a pistol, which the lieutenant thrust aside as it was being discharged—thus escaping with his life and succeeding also in expelling the savage. The Indians now took a position at a window, and there shot Stenton as he was in the act of rising from bed. Rushing from the house, the wounded man ran for a mile and dropped down a corpse. His wife and two children, meanwhile, had secreted themselves in the cellar, where they were fired upon three times, but without being struck. Capt. Wetterhold, despite his suffering, dragged himself to a window, through which he shot one of the savages in the act of applying a torch to the house. Hereupon taking up the dead body of their comrade the besiegers withdrew. Having on their retreat plundered the house of James Allen, they attacked Andrew Hazlitt's, where they shot and scalped a man, shot Hazlitt himself after a bold defence, and then tomahawked his fugitive wife and two children in a barbarous mannner. Finally they set fire to his house, and next to that of Philip Kratzer, and crossing the Lehigh, made off with their spoils for the mountain.

Intelligence of this sad affair reached Bethlehem a few hours after its occurrence, whereupon a small armed force was sent to the scene of the surprise to bring the wounded men to town for surgical treatment. So it came to pass, that Captain Wetterhold breathed his last at The Crown on the 9th of October, and was buried next day in the grave-yard near by. We find the following charge on record in The Crown's day-book under date of 10th October, 1763:

	l.	s.	d.
"Capt. Jacob Wetterhold, Dr. to			
1 pint wine, ...		1	2
For 1 pint beer, ...			2½
" eating and drinking for his attendants, ...		2	0
" oats and pasture for 2 horses, .		3	0
" a shroud, ...		6	0
" ferriage for his attendants ten times, ...		2	0
		14	4½"

Sergeant McGuire lay upwards of three weeks at the Inn under the care of Dr. Otto. It is stated that the body of the Captain's servant who was the first to fall at Stenton's, was also brought to Bethlehem, and along with another victim was interred on what was then known as "the Burnside Farm (now William Lerch's), on the Menagassi. Sergeant McGuire's charges at the Inn, dated 8th November, 1763, are as follows:

	l.	s.	d.
"Sergeant L. McGuire, Dr.			
For 4 half pints wine, . . .		2	4
" beer and cider royal, . .			9
" cash, ...		7	6
" his wife's diet for eight days,		10	0
" 2 breakfasts, . . .		1	0
" 1 horse at hay, . . .			8
" 25 days' diet and attendance at 1*s*. 9*d*. per day, . .	2	3	9
	3	6	0"

This bold foray struck terror, as well it might, into the neighborhood, and next day The Crown Inn swarmed with refugees from Allen and Lehigh townships. A panic also seized the inhabitants of Saucon valley, who crowded its precincts on two occasions between the 11th and 18th of the eventful month, while the arrival of several companies of mounted men from Bucks in that interval, heightened the general confusion at the house. It was late in December before the last of the fugitives had returned to their homes. One of their number, a woman, died at The Crown on the 19th of October, and was buried on the hill.

On the 10th of September, prior to the occurrences just narrated, there set out from Bethlehem, via The Crown for Philadelphia, a "stage-wagon" for the convenience of public travel,—it being the first of those successive generations of "swift and sure" lines of coaches, which tortured mortal flesh, until their utter extinction by steam. George Klein was the father of this enterprise, which must needs have been a humble one, in order to be prophetic of higher creations in times to come. John Koppel drove the wagon for 40*l.* per annum. But as his coach was seldom full he prudently engaged in the additional transportation of freight, carrying either groceries for the store, or train-oil for the tanner, or iron for the nail-smith, or wool for the clothier. We note, as indicative of an early Israelitish migration into Northampton, that Koppel, in June of 1763, conveyed household furniture for Mordecai, a Jew of Easton, and for Jacob, a Jew of Allentown, to those respective seats of traffic. Despite this mode of supplementing a cargo, and a charge of ten shillings for a passenger over the route, the enterprise sank 82*l.* 12*s.* 7*d.* in the first year of its existence. Nevertheless, for many years, hereafter the curiosity of the *habitués* of the Inn was more than ordinarily exercised on Friday afternoon of every week, on the return of the stage-wagon from the capital.*

The month of November of 1763, proved an exciting one at Bethlehem and at The Crown, as the popular feeling against the Moravian Indians (who had made that place their asylum since November of 1755, consequent upon the late inroads) was then culminating. To such a degree did prejudice against another race then blind men's reason, that Government hastened to order the removal of this unfortunate people for safe-keeping to the capital. Accordingly in the afternoon of the eighth of the aforementioned month, the Moravian Indians (there were one hundred and twenty-one, men, women and children) rendezvoused at Lischer's, preparatory to their exodus. This was a memorable day at the Inn. The following record, the last relating to this eventful administration, points to the return of these exiles in March of 1765, and to their subsequent transfer to Wyalusing on the Susquehanna:

*In November of 1764, Klein sold out to John Francis Oberlin, the latter paying him for the wagon, a pale mare, a sorrel (*der Fuchs*), a roan (*der Bock*), a bay, harness, chains, an axe, a tar-bucket, and eight sacks for oats--52*l.* Penna. cy. In Henry Miller's Almanac for 1765, in a "specification of the times of the arrival and departure of post-riders, mail-coaches and market-boats, at and from Philadelphia," we find the following announcement—"Every Thursday morning a mail-coach leaves Race St. for Bethlehem, and returns on Tuesday to Philadelphia."

		l.	s.	d.
"1 April 1765.	Joseph Fox, Esq., Dr.			
	For an order of Thomas Apty for keeping horses when he came with ye Indians from Philadelphia, viz.:			
	For 8 horses 5 days at hay, . .	2	13	4
	" 7 " 7 " . .	3	5	4
	" oats for "		16	6
	" ferriage, ...		3	2
		6	18	4"

It remains to be stated that the Inn made a deficit of 41*l.* 10*s.* 9½*d.* for the year ending 1st April, 1765,—that Mr. Lischer on the 19th of that month exchanged its responsibilities for those of The Rose on the Barony—that thence he was called in 1772, to take charge of the Nazareth Inn, and that he died at Nazareth in May of 1782.

Ephraim Culver succeeded to The Crown on the 20th day of April, 1765,—that being the date of this his second coronation,—and swayed the scepter at the Inn for a period of five years, which flowed gently down the stream of time. It was to a remarkable degree, what we might characterize as an introspective life which host and hostelry led during this incumbency, in the absence of Indian wars, and despite an ominous movement in the Province and her sister colonies, which augured no good to the

Proprietary Government and to the Seigniory of Windsor. The brief records of the house, accordingly, as we may expect, refer almost exclusively to its economy, thereby, however, acquainting us with much that is pleasant to know. Thus, for instance, the following inventory of stock taken on the 19th of April, of the last mentioned year, throws a clear light upon what were the appurtenances of the Inn at that date. "There is on hand at The Crown, this day—

		l.	s.	d.
Kitchen Furniture, .	valued at	17	17	11
Drinking vessels, . .	"	6	18	9
Tea and coffee vessels, . .	"	6	2	10
Earthen ware, . . .	"	1	11	1
Bedding, ...	"	32	10	0
Linen, ...	"	3	2	4
Sundry utensils, . . .	"	11	13	6
Casks, &c., . . .	"	5	11	6
Tools at ye barn and stable, .	"	2	4	10
Garden tools, . . .	"	2	3	2
		89	15	11"

A second record testifies to the character of the literature which was provided by the host for the intellectual entertainment of his guests. It reads thus: "March 21st, 1766, paid Messrs. Franklin and Hall, for the newspapers for last year, 10*s*. 7*d*." And again, "March 17th, 1767, paid Henry Miller, for the newspapers for two years past, 12*s*."

In 1767, our Inn was taxed 5*l.* 18*s.* 6*d.* for the Province, and 2*l.* 7*s.* 6*d.* for the county. On the 19th of April, of the following year, its premises were for a time jeopardized by a bush-fire, that swept down the mountain; but neighbors coming to the rescue, the enemy was subdued, at a cost of one and threepence, for rum, to the Inn. Finally, an examination of accounts of the house by duly authorized auditors, on the 18th of April, 1770, discovered among the rest, that the sum total of sundry small outstanding debts due to the Crown amounted to 20*l.* 2*s.* 8*d.*

We left the Bethlehem Ferry in the hands of Francis Steup, in the winter of 1761. On the dissolution of the Economy it was united with the Inn, and managed for one year by Augustus H. Franke, in consideration of 23*l.* per annum, in addition to his and his wife's board, reckoned at seven and sixpence per week for each. He was assisted by Peter Petersen, who is charged on one and the same day with one pair of leather breeches, new, 16*s.* 9*d.*, and one pair ditto, old, 5*s.*, whence we infer that his position was a wearing one and no sinecure. Franke's receipts for the year ending the 27th of March, 1763, amounted to 165*l.* 11*d.*, of which sum 73*l.* 18*s.* 6½*d.*, were net proceeds, which goes to prove that the Ferry (then booked at 185*l.* 18*s.* 4*d.*, including wharves, flat, rope, and shelter belonging thereto, four canoes and chains), was a desirable investment.*

Valentine Fuehrer (whom we shall meet again in the course of this narrative) succeeded Franke as ferryman, and continued a lodger at the Crown, as his predecessors had been, until the completion of the Ferry House,† erected in the autumn of 1765, at the

---

* The rates of ferriage at this time may in part be deduced from the following item, dated "31st October, 1762." The Bethlehem Farm, Frederic Beckel, farmer, Dr. to the Ferry:

	l.	s.	p.
For ferrying 1 wagon, ...	0	5	0
" " 1 horse three times, ...	0	1	0
" " 344 sheep, ...	0	18	9½
" " the sisters who worked in harvest one week and a half, back and forth, .	4	0	1½
	5	4	11

† The Ferry-house stood near the site of the house of entertainment enigmatically ycleped first, The Mondray House, but now The Exchange, until work at the Lehigh Valley Railroad in 1853, caused its removal. After the Bethlehem Ferry had been superseded by a bridge (in 1794), the house was occupied by the successive toll-men in the employ of the Bridge Company--first by Valentine Fuehrer, next in 1801 by Peter Rose (he had served under Braddock), and after him successively by John Stotz, Massa Warner (he died in the house in May of 1824), Benjamin Warner, John Adam Luckenbach and Daniel Lawall. In 1842, subsequent to the erection of a toll-house at the northern terminus of the present bridge, Daniel Desh came into possession of the ferry-house, and occupied it for six years. He then rented it to Jacob Werst. The last occupant was one "Dutch John," who also removed

southern terminus of the ferry. This he occupied on the 17th of October of that year. It was built by David Kunz, from Moravia, carpenter, at a cost of 19*l.* 17*s.* 4½*d.*

Here it behooves us to present to the reader the following:

Schedule of rates of Ferriage at the Bethlehem Ferry, January, 1767.

	l.	s.	d.
For a loaded wagon and four horses, . .		3	0
" an empty do. do. . .		2	0
" a loaded wagon and two horses, . .		2	6
" an empty do. do. . .		2	6
" a carriage with four wheels and two horses, ...		2	6
" a chair and one horse, . . .		1	6
" a do. two horses, . . .		1	10
" a sled and four do. . . .		3	0
" a do. two do. . . .		1	6
" a do. one horse, . . .		1	2
" a single horse, ...			6
" a number of horses, each . . .			4
" a footman, ...	2 coppers.		
" a single ox or cow, ...			6
" a number of oxen or cows, each . .			4
" a single sheep, hog or calf, each . .	2 coppers.		
" ten head of the same, . . .		1	0"

---

the building, and from its sound timbers constructed a dwelling, which he located on the river's bank, near its old haunt.

Accompanying this schedule was the following

"ADVERTISEMENT.

"All such persons as bring wheat, rye, Indian corn, and buckwheat, to the grist-mill at Bethlehem, for grinding, are free of ferriage, provided they observe the following regulations, to wit:

One horse with two bushels of wheat, rye, or Indian corn.
One do. " three do. buckwheat.

One wagon and four horses with		twenty bushels of wheat.	
One do.	" two do.	" fifteen	do.
One cart	" do.	" twelve	do.
One do.	" one do.	" eight	do.
One sled	" two do.	" twelve	do.
One do.	" one do.	" six	do.

Besides the above-mentioned quantities of grain, all kinds of provisions brought for sale in Bethlehem are allowed on the same wagon or horse. Furthermore, all persons that come to church at Bethlehem on Sundays or holydays are ferriage free, provided they do not come for the purpose of transacting business, or carry parcels,—in which case they are to pay the usual rates."

There is an event in Mr. Fuehrer's life as ferryman, which it is proper to state at this point in our history. When Governor John Penn was tarrying a few days at Bethlehem, in April of 1768 (he was wont to visit the Allens, of Allentown, Ann, his wife, being a daughter of the Chief Justice), it so happened on the twenty-seventh of the month, that the men of the village were fishing for shad (it was the height of what we might style the Devonian age, and one hundred and five years before the introduction of black bass by an overland route*), after the Indian mode of taking that excellent fish.†

* "Last night about one o'clock," we quote from the Bethlehem Daily Times of 13th June, a. c., "two tanks containing 400 black bass from the Potomac at Harper's Ferry arrived at the Freight Depot of the N. P. R. R.—a large number of beautiful fish ——— dead." "Four hundred piscatorial corpses of piscatorial hopes entertained by the public-spirited gentlemen who had been active in setting on foot the black bass movement." *Ibid.*

† "As soon as the shad (*Scha-wa-nam-meek*) *i. e.*, the *South-fish*, compounded of *Scha-wa-ne-u*, south, hence Shawano,—and *Na-mees* fish, in their annual migration from the tropical seas, run up the rivers along the Atlantic coast to deposit their spawn, the Indians assemble for the fishery. Having built a dam across the stream with walls converging into a pound at its center, they twist a cable of grape-vines, loading it down with brush secured at intervals of from ten to fifteen feet. This barrier is stretched from shore to shore, perhaps a mile above the wier and being held in position by Indians in canoes, is towed down the river. The frightened fish are driven before it, and by men, stationed on the walls, into the pound, and there taken by hand. The Delawares called March, the "shad-month." *Memorials of the Moravian Church, vol.* 2. Shad were taken abundantly in this way, by the Moravians at Bethlehem, in the Lehigh below the Simpson Tract, until improvements were made in the bed of the river by the Lehigh Coal and Navigation Company, about 1820. The largest catch on record,—6th May, 1772—numbered 5,300.

Now, the Governor was desirous of witnessing the catch. Hereupon Mr. Fuehrer fitted up his best batteau, and having taken his Honor on board from a spit on the Sand Island, rowed him within the magic circle described by the grape-vine cable, into the pound, below the wier, and, in short, to every available point of view (the Governor, we are told by Mr. Watson, was very near-sighted), much to his gratification. His lady and her attendants, meanwhile, watched the exciting sport from the heights of Nisky Hill.

When Ephraim Culver retired from the Crown in April of 1771, Valentine Fuehrer was still at his post at the ferry. Mr. Culver in April of 1772 became a resident of the charming hamlet of Schoeneck on the Barony — there married widow Claus for his third wife — and died at Bethlehem in March of 1775.

A division of the estates held by the Moravian Church in the Province of Pennsylvania completed about this time, led to a transfer of The Crown Inn and the adjacent lands to the Society at Bethlehem. Hereupon that body let the hostelry (it was booked at 230*l.*, the Ferry at 50*l.*) and a few acres of land contiguous, to Augustus H. Franke, a native of Eckersheim in Lower Lusatia (he had immigrated in 1754) at an annual rental of 30*l.* He took possession on the 6th of April, 1771, and assisted by his wife, Mary Magdalene m. n. Steiner, managed both the house and the farm for his own emolument until the same day of April, 1778.

During this incumbency, although it fell in that memorable period in which her transatlantic colonies asserted, and then, by an appeal to arms, established their independence of Great Britain—no events of importance occurred at the Inn but what were intimately related with events which rightfully belong to the history of the town of Bethlehem. Passing these over, accordingly, as things known to even careless readers of Moravian history, it may be stated, in conclusion, that there were no more exciting days at the Crown, than the days of the week after the defeat of the Americans at Chadd's Ford (11th September, 1777), when soldiers, statesmen and civilians fled from before the British lion in Philadelphia, past our house's royal emblem and across its ferry to Bethlehem;—a hegira, which we may suppose has no parallel in precipitancy save that of Mohammed, and none in the promiscuousness of its elements, excepting that of the first Bull Run. Valentine Fuehrer was ferryman at this critical juncture,—in fact, until the expiration of Franke's lease.*

* We learn from 2 Penn'a Archives, p. 288, that John G. Jungman, who had been obliged by reason of a severe hypochondriac disorder to return to Bethlehem from the Indian mission, led by the advice of his

He was also the thirteenth landlord at The Crown, if such continued to be the name of our Inn, at a time when popular feeling throughout the land had been enlisted in an indiscriminate crusade against the insignia of royalty. Of Mr. Fuehrer, we know the following. He was born July 17th, 1732, in upper Esopus on the confines of Kaatskill, where his father Christian Fuehrer was a deacon in the Reformed Church of the Palatine settlers. Becoming attatched to Moravian principles through Moravian missionaries, who, in the course of their spiritual labors among some Mohegans at Stissik, near Rhinebeck, occasionally visited the Germans located in that region of country, young Fuehrer on attaining his majority, accompained Martin Mack, to Bethlehem, the new home of his choice. This was in March of 1745. In August of 1755, he married Margaret Elizabeth, a daughter of George and Christiana Loesch of Tulpehocken, and having done much service for the Economy in the capacity of a farmer, on its dissolution, was appointed, as we have seen, ferryman at the Bethlehem Ferry. It was in the fifteenth year of his incumbency there,

---

physicians, who thought bodily exercise very beneficial to him, "worked at the ferry for three years, during the time when the hospitals and other parts of the army were constantly passing and repassing the Lehigh."

and on the 6th of April, 1778, that he was called to take charge of The Crown, with a salary of 30*l.* per annum. Fuehrer was its responsible head until the 1st of July, 1791,—for full thirteen years,*—in the first six of which he also superintended the management of the ferry. When Sullivan had his headquarters at Easton, at the time he was fitting out an expedition against the Indians of the Six Nations, Fuehrer's flat was impressed into the public service and taken to Easton, to assist in transporting troops and munitions of war across the Delaware. This was in June of 1779. Massa Warner, a son of Daniel and Bethiah Warner,—born in the town of Hebron,

---

* During this period the Moravian Seminary for Young Ladies at Bethlehem (after having been established in October of 1785), set out upon a career of usefulness in behalf of the amelioration of womankind, in which it has persevered, undaunted, for almost a full century. In this period, then, a new element began to appear in and to lend charms (year after year more decidedly) to the beautiful environs of Bethlehem, as well to the nether as to the upper shore of Lehigh, as during Fuehrer's incumbency at The Crown, the Simpson Tract was for the first time trodden by the feet of denizens of the aforementioned venerable Institution. * * * * But this element, with the lapse of time, has grown mighty toward giving character to Bethlehem and its adjacents,—whether the maidens in double file and under the wholesome restraint of a quasi-military discipline, move demurely in dense squadrons through the precincts of the borough,—or whether, when without its limits, they break line, and following the bent of their happy natures roam light-heartedly and with graceful *abandon* through the sylvan remains of the historic scenes of which we write.

Litchfield county, Connecticut,—was the next ferry-man in the succession, in the interval between 1st of April, 1784, and the aforementioned 1st of July, 1791. But his salary was 70*l.* per annum, and his perquisites were a home in the ferry-house, two cords of wood every season, and hay and pasture for a cow.

Mr. Fuehrer, it has been stated, spent thirteen years of his life as landlord of The Crown. The events of interest which occurred at the old house, or which, occurring elsewhere during this period, nevertheless affected its status, may be rehearsed briefly and in order as follows. In the early winter of 1780, the Lehigh was closed for seven weeks continuously, and as the ice permitted the transit of even heavily laden wains, there could not possibly be any receipts for ferriage for that time. Washington, accompanied by two aids (the General was on his way to headquarters at Newburg), passed the 25th day of July, 1782, at Bethlehem. According to the late Mr. Frederick Fuehrer's statement (he was the fifth son of Valentine and Margaret Fuehrer and having been born in the ferry-house in September, 1768, was in the fifteenth year of his age, when Washington was at Bethlehem), the General passed the night of the 24th of July, at his father's, and on retiring pleasantly sought to impress the people of the house with an idea of the heighth of his person by reaching his hand into a ring suspended from a staple in the ceiling which was inaccessible by men of ordinary stature.

On the 8th of November, 1782, a few weeks prior to the signing of provisional articles of peace at Paris, several companies of a Continental regiment en route from Lancaster to Wilmington, were quartered at The Crown. This was its last occupation by patriot troops, as hostilities between the belligerents ceased in the following January. But when a definitive treaty of peace was concluded at Brussels in September of 1783, the house and the tract on which it stood, together with divers other estates personal and real, passed completely under the jurisdiction of the new Republic.

John George Stoll, the ninth child of John J. and Ann. M. Stoll, of Balgheim, Principality of Oettinger (Mr. Stoll had immigrated in 1749), and Rosina, his wife, succeeded to the Crown, on the 1st of July, 1791. This is the same John Stoll, who while saw-miller at Bethlehem (he spent twenty years of his life in that romantic little world near the outlet of the Menagassi, where since 1743, amid alders and willows, have been heard the hum of the waterfall and the sound of the busy saw) rendered professional services to the United States of America, to the amount of 9*l.*, he having sawed three hundred feet of timber for the Continental Stable, located in November of 1799, on John Lerch's farm* in Allen township. From the mill, Mr. Stoll, by an easy gradation, passed over the river to The Crown. He presided over its fortunes until the 30th of May, 1792. Mr. Stoll died at Bethlehem, in March of 1801.†

George Schindler, from the village of Zauchtenthal, Moravia, linen-weaver (he had immigrated in the spring of 1754), and Mary Magdalene, third daughter of Conrad and Catharine Wetzel, of Goshenhoppen, his wife, were installed at the Crown on the last day of May 1792, and administered its affairs to the 31st of October, 1794. On that day the house closed its public career, "disappearing without glory," from the ranks of its fellow inns. The Ferry, however (Valentine Fuehrer had managed it since his retirement from the Crown), had

---

*Lerch's farm of 150 acres situate on the Lehigh, had been conveyed to John Lerch in 1773 by Anthony Lerch, the elder, of Lower Saucon, it being a part of a tract of 1,800 acres of land in the forks of Hockendauqua, held by Wm. Allen in 1740—conveyed to William Parsons in 1754, conveyed by Parsons to Richard Peters, and by Peters to Wm. Allen, and Joseph Turner, in the aforementioned year; one hundred and fifty acres of which great tract were sold in 1761, to John Stenton, by him to John Jennings, and by Jennings, in 1770, to Anthony Lerch. John Lerch, of Bethlehem, merchant, is a grandson of the aforementioned John Lerch.

†Mr. Andrew G. Kern, of Nazareth, the venerable Moravian antiquary, now in the 79th year of his age, is a grandson of John G. Stoll.

been abandoned on the 27th of September, of the last mentioned year; whereupon the veteran ferryman received a gratuity of 10*l.* in consideration of his past services.

In January of 1792, the Moravians first agitated the question of connecting the Simpson Tract with their town by means of a bridge. Having been empowered to do so by an Act of Assembly, that was passed 3d April, 1792, under the hand and seal of Thomas Mifflin, the then Governor of the Commonwealth of Pennsylvania, said act providing for "the establishing and building of a bridge across the Lehigh at Bethlehem," and empowering John Schropp of that place to build said bridge,—vesting, moreover, the same when built, in "him, his heirs and assigns forever"—work was commenced at the structure in the spring of 1794. Despite some delays occasioned by freshets in the river, the bridge*

* This bridge was an uncovered one, and was built of hemlock timber, cut in what was then called "the little Spruce Swamp," between Panther Creek and the Nesquehoning, in Carbon county. It was constructed at a cost of $7,800, which sum was divided among stockholders, whom, Mr. Schropp, agreeably to the tenor of the act, had associated with himself; shares being issued at $100. In 1816, this bridge being found imperfect, was removed, and its place taken by a more durable one (also uncovered), which rested upon four stone piers, furnished with ice-breakers. It was opened for travel 19th October, 1816. In April of 1827, the present "Bethlehem Bridge Company" was incorporated by charter and organized. The bridge of 1816 was carried

was opened for travel on the 19th day of September next ensuing,—whereupon, and since that time (save temporarily, as, for instance, in 1816 and again in 1841), the historic Simpson Tract has been connected more closely and more effectually with Bethlehem, than ever it was by stoutest shroud hawser of ninety fathoms.

George Schindler, died at Bethlehem in March of 1809. His widow survived him until April of 1825.* Thus passed away the last host and hostess of the old Crown Inn.

This narrative would be incomplete, were it to close here. The transformation of the Simpson Tract and of the lands adjacent, so that their condition became by insensible steps very different from that in which we found it in the days of Conrad Ruetschi, and very different from what it is remembered to

---

away by the great freshet which swept the valley of the Lehigh, in January of 1841. It was superseded in the same year by the present covered one, which, with the lapse of years, is very perceptibly growing old.

*But how she spent her widowhood in a cottage on Market street, earning a livelihood by spinning and by boarding pupils of the Bethlehem school; how, like other exemplary old ladies of whom we read in books, she had a rush bottomed chair, an eight-day clock and a tortoise-shell cat; how she became a favorite with the children of the town, by inviting them to "vespers," when she would always serve up "*et-was frisch gebackenes*," and how in consequence she was called by the endearing appellation of Mammy, first by them, and then by every one, until the day of her death, the reader may learn in full, by consulting "Bethlehem and Bethlehem School," by C. B. Mortimer.

have been but a quarter of a century ago,—and the fate of the old house whose name is borne on the title page of this tribute to its memory, must necessarily be traced, if even briefly. In order to do this, we must return to the year 1769, which was the seventh year after the dissolution of the Bethlehem Economy. In February, of that year, the Moravians laid out two farms on their lands lying south of the Lehigh river, and let them to tenants. The improvements on the upper Ysselstein place, served as a nucleus for the larger of the two, including, furthermore, the clearings that had been made about the Inn. This farm, first known in official records as "Die Plantage beym Gasthaus zur Krone," was occupied in 1769 by Conrad Ernst, from Wald Angelloch, in the Palatinate, and Ann C., daughter of Sebastian H. and Ann Catharine Knauss, of Emmaus, his wife.* The second farm, called "The Weygandt Farm" (its improvements gradually clustered around a clearing made by Cornelius Weygandt† on a

* The old log dwelling, which in 1849, was superseded by one of brick (the same that at present contains offices in the freight department of the Lehigh Valley Railroad Co.), was erected in 1765, and subsequently occupied by Ernst and the successive tenants of this farm.

† Cornelius Weygandt, was born in March of 1713, in Osthofen, in the Palatinate. He died in October of 1799, and lies buried in the grave-yard of the Schœneck Church, in Bushkill township. Some of his descendants reside in Easton. He doubtless built the ancient farm-house, which stands in the rear of Bishopthorpe, circa 1759.

tract of eighty acres of mountain land purchased by George Hartmann, 1744), was let to Marx Kieffer* in April of the aforementioned year 1769. Ernst was succeeded in April of 1779, by John Luckenbach, last from Locust Grove, in Upper Saucon township. John Luckenbach† was succeeded in April of 1786 by his son, John Adam; he in 1810 by his son, John David, and he in 1845 by his son, Thomas David. Thus, because of its occupancy for many years by the members of that family, the farm came to be called "The Luckenbach Farm."

Kieffer dying in 1791 (during his tenancy, there were some of Burgoyne's Brunswickers, then on parol, quartered at his house), was succeeded by John Christian Clevel,‡ he, about 1810, by John Hoffert, and he in 1834 by his son, Samuel Hoffert. This farm was known during the last years of its tenure by the Moravians as "the Hoffert Farm."§

Subsequent to the Revolution (about 1786), the

---

* Marx Kieffer was from Nielingen, in Durlach, and was blacksmith at the Shamokin mission when the Indian war broke out, in November of 1755.

† John Luckenbach, the ancestor of the family of that name at Bethlehem, died in June of 1810. John Adam died in April of 1842, and John David, in August of 1850.

‡ John C. Clevel, a son of George Clevel, was born in September of 1754, in Plainfield township. He died near Bethlehem, in June of 1827.

§ John Hoffert died in October of 1837. Samuel Hoffert died in March of 1864.

THE FUEHRER HOUSE (The Old Crown Inn), 1854.
North Front—showing the room on the first floor in the northwest angle of the house, in which Washington passed the night of the 24th and 25th of July, 1782. After a sketch taken by R. A. Grider.

"Luckenbach Farm," which at that time extended at points to the west of the Emmaus road, was divided,—and one hundred acres on its south side were made into a third farm—this being given in tenancy to Stoffel Wiener. Wiener was succeeded by Jacob Jacobi, in 1805, and he, in 1815 by his son, Jacob Jacobi, Jr. This farm was last known as "the Jacobi Farm."*

Frederic Fuehrer commenced the fourth of the Moravian Farms situate on the south bank of the Lehigh, about 1794, and thereupon occupied the old Crown Inn. Thus the hostelry became a farm-house. In it Valentine Fuehrer spent the last years of his life. But in his old age the ferryman's vision grew dim until he became totally blind. Then like Oedipus, he was led about by children and children's children. He died on the 12th of January, 1808. Frederic Fuehrer, who had developed the new farm, until its cultivated fields extended westward to the borders of "The Hoffert Farm," died at Bethlehem, on the 1st of March, 1849. But on the very day of his death, there was felled a white pine (it had well nigh been uprooted by a storm), which he when a young man, had planted in the garden hard by the old Crown,—saying as he set out the sapling, that he desired for it a prosperous growth, and wood

* Stoffel Wiener died circa 1845, in the neighborhood of Bethlehem, upwards of ninety years of age. Jacob Jacobi died circa 1815; Jacob Jacobi, Jr., in 1869.

from its trunk for a coffin, when he should come to die.—Joseph Fuehrer, a son of Frederick Fuehrer was the tenant on "The Fuehrer Farm," when in 1847 it was sold by the Moravians. Now all these farms stretched into the Simpson Tract, and in the last year of their tenure by their original holders contained jointly full five hundred acres of arable land.

Reckoning from the year in which the house of which we write ceased to be an Inn, we count forty years for the duration of what may, not inappropriately, be termed the bucolic age of the tract on which it stood;—an age, in which a Sabbath calm brooded over the husbandman's acres and the fruits of the husbandman's toil,—when no sound invaded the universal stillness of that enchanted world by day, save the lowing of herds, or the ring of the mower's scythe, or the hum of honey-bees; and none by night, but the clink of hopples in the clover, or the distant watch-dog's bark echoed along the mountain. Then Heaven smiled and the seven planets shed sweet influence upon fallow and orchard,—upon seeded field and standing corn; granting, moreover, rich increase to flocks and healthful progeny to men. No plague, then, of blight or mildew, of murrain or pestilence, as the moon spake kindly oracles and the mystic signs of the zodiac taught men how to avert dreaded disease. Thus passed the years and months of this bucolic age,—fallow-month, hay-month, autumn-month, winter-month and Christ-month,—each, in turn, pouring out treasures from its horn of plenty, until, it appeared as though Saturn purposed to return to the earth and take up his abode with the race of articulate men.

Meanwhile, in the wilds of upper Northampton, where the Lehigh, yet an untamed mountain-stream, frets in its rocky bed, brave spirits were fighting the powers of Nature,—as men of old fought dragons—if, peradventure, they might wrest from her enchantments and share with their fellow-men, the treasures she fain would keep to herself in her savage solitudes. It needed brave spirits, indeed, to pioneer the way for that inexhaustible traffic which now pours a continuous stream of merchandise through its great artery in the valley of the Lehigh, to the emporiums of the western world. Such spirits were Cist, Miner, White, Hazard and Hauto, whose names are inscribed upon the title-page of the almost fabulous history of anthracite coal. Exchanging the amenities of civilized life, for the hardships and denials of life in the woods, these men toiled year after year in a howling wilderness (on the land and in the water), hewing roads through its sombre forests, clearing its river's channel of obstructions, hoping against hope and yet persevering, until they had accomplished what they designed should not be left undone. Thus they slew the dragon.

16

Now what these and their fellows eventually effected towards bringing anthracite to market, is as well known to the reader, as its recital would be irrelevant to the subject of this narrative; still, it is proper to state, that towards evening of the 3d of August, 1813, there swept down the Lehigh, past the Simpson Tract and the old Crown Inn, a craft such as had never before been borne upon its waters. This craft was an "ark" (the first of many that followed in its wake), laden with twenty-four tons of coal, on her way to Philadelphia,—a rude hulk of hemlock timbers, forsooth, carrying a mere handful of fossil fuel, and yet prophetic of fleets of argosies, which in time to come should sweep past the site of the olden hostelry, all freighted heavily with the spoils of a long-past carboniferous age.

In 1820 "The Lehigh Coal Company" (formed in 1792) and the "Lehigh Navigation Company" (formed in 1818) merged their interests into a new organization with the corporate title eventually of "The Lehigh Coal and Navigation Company." This company found the river, whose name henceforth became identified with its varied enterprises, well fitted up with locks and dams for flooding its channel in seasons of shoal water, by which means coal was as heretofore sent to market in arks, until the summer of 1829. It was then that navigation in the newly completed canal was opened. Within a twelvemonth thereafter, thirty thousand tons of anthracite from Bear Mountain, passed over this new highway southward into consumers' hands — Such was the dawn of a modern carboniferous age.

Now all these operations in mining of coal and in behalf of its transportation down the valley of the Lehigh, begat a spirit of unrest which followed the courses of that river to its outlet. Men began to ponder a movement which was rapidly infusing the vigor of a new life into a hitherto unheeded region of country, and as they pondered and speculated, — there were some who in vision beheld coal wedded to iron, and the offspring of this union—gold. Hereupon the rod of witch-hazel in the diviner's hand was made to point out the subterranean abode of the king of metals. Thus iron was found; and then iron was smelted by the agency of anthracite in stacks with flaming throats. This triumph of metallurgy was first achieved at Catasauqua in the summer of 1840. Seven years subsequent to that great event, the Moravians sold their farms. It grieved them, we ween, to see hereditary acres, which were long associated in their minds with the days of the Bethlehem Economy and the patriarchal rule of Spangenberg, pass from their hands; but they hearkened to the words of far-sighted men who contended that it would be madness to attempt to rescue them from the high-tide which in that dayspring of modern improvement was setting in towards their borders, threatening to overwhelm in ruin all things that refused to bow before its irresistible progress. Hence they were sold, to wit: five hundred acres and upwards on the south side of the Lehigh alone, including the Simpson Tract, and the old building which in the days of the Penns and of loyalty to the House of Hanover, had been The Crown Inn. From the sale of these lands, date the beginnings of that change which has so steadily and so marvellously been transforming the south bank of the Lehigh, opposite the old Moravian settlement of Bethlehem, down to the present day. The first impetus was given it, perhaps, when in 1852, works for the manufacture of zinc were erected in the newly laid out town of Augusta,—which town, as it grew (and it grew rapidly on the completion of the Lehigh Valley and North Pennsylvania Railroads), changed its name frequently, being called sometime Wetherill, and sometime Bethlehem South—but eventually, the borough of South Bethlehem. How this vigorous town grew from year to year, as it took within its borders new portions of the old Moravain farms, adding new peoples too, as often as new works for the production of zinc and iron and brass, were established;—and how the railroads became effectual in bringing trade and traffic of all kinds, as well as coal and iron and gold, to its bustling market—need not here be rehearsed. All this is well known to the reader. He, too, may predict what eventually, in all probability, will be the extent and character of the ambitious town that has supplanted the Moravian farms and the site of the old Crown Inn. With this we are not concerned; but, instead, with the fate of the old ferry-house, which was demolished to make way for the track of the Lehigh Valley Railroad; and with that of the old Crown Inn, which was removed from its lookout, in the summer of 1857—it being proven that it stood in the very bed of the North Pennsylvania Railroad—whereupon it was sold for the paltry sum of thirty dollars—itself and all its historical reminiscences; and having been given over gently to the axe and the saw, its well preserved remains were made to do service in houses of modern structure.

Thus the old Crown Inn, in part, has entered upon a new career, in which it may make history for the delight of some future recorder or antiquarian, if not, peradventure, for the edification of future readers of olden time lore.

APPENDIX,

CONTAINING DIVERSE MATTER SUPPLEMENTARY TO THE FOREGOING HISTORY.

I.

TREATING OF THE PLANTATIONS IN THE NEIGHBORHOOD OF BETHLEHEM, PRIOR TO 1741.

Three plantations, lying at intervals within a stretch of four miles on the south bank of the Lehigh, were the only indications of the white man's presence in their neighborhood, when the Moravians began to build Bethlehem. Two miles above them in a bend of the river was the "Jennings' Farm," a choice parcel of 200 acres which had been confirmed to Solomon Jennings (he was one of the "three walkers"), in the spring of 1736, by William Allen, and which after being patented, "was holden of the Proprietaries as part of their Manor of Fermor or the Drylands in free and common soccage, on paying in lieu of all other services to them or their successors at the town of Easton, on the first day of March annually, one silver shilling for each one hundred acres." This farm, on being exposed at public sale after the demise of old Solomon (he deceased 16th February, 1757) by his executors, John Jennings, Nicholas Scull of the county of Berks, tavern-keeper, and Isaiah Jennings, was bought by Jacob Geisinger of Saucon township, yeoman, together with 164 acres additional, for 1,500*l.* Pennsylvania currency, and confirmed to him by indenture bearing date of 1st June, 1764. It is held by his descendants to the present day.

Near the mouth of Saucon creek was the "Irish Farm," whose history is given fully elsewhere.

The third plantation was the "Ysselstein Farm," lying due east of the Simpson tract and stretching down the river four hundred and four perches to the west line of the "Irish Farm,"—including two separate purchases, to wit: a tract of 178 acres and an island of 10 acres (now held by the Bethlehem Iron Company), which had been surveyed to David Potts of the County of Bucks, yeoman, in July of 1734, by him assigned to Isaac Ysselstein in December of 1738, to whom they were deeded by William Allen in December of 1740, for the consideration of 100*l.* Pennsylvania currency—and a second tract of 75 acres, due east of and adjoining the first, which was conveyed to the aforesaid Ysselstein by Nathaniel Irish, in December of 1739, for 26*l.* 5*s.* Pennsylvania currency. This plantation was purchased by the Moravians of widow Ysselstein in 1749.* Of the original holder we know the following:

Isaac Martens Ysselstein, was of Low Dutch parentage, and resided in Esopus in 1725, in which year he married Rachel Bogart. From Esopus he removed to the Dutch settlement of Claverack (Clover Field), on the east shore of Hudson's river, and thence to Marbletown, six miles west from Kingston on "the old Mine road." Allured by the prospect of cheap and fertile lands which were being thrown into the market by speculators in the Forks of the Delaware, even prior to the extinction of the Indian claim, he followed others of his countrymen into the new land of promise, and purchased, as we have seen, on the south bank of Lecha, building himself a cabin just over against the ford where Marshall and Yeates, the walkers, and their Indian companions Combash, Tom and Tuneam had ridden their horses through the stream, in the afternoon of the memorable 19th September, 1737. His family at that time consisted of four daughters, a negress, and a servant man, Jacobus van der Merck. But one night, it was in the spring of 1739, the treacherous river suddenly rose and overflowing its banks, swept away the cabin of the settler, and the timbers he was squaring for a more substantial homestead and for the housing of his cattle. So impetuous was the angry flood that the inmates of the doomed house barely escaped with their lives to higher ground. This is the first freshet in the Lehigh on record, it being the one which served as a standard of comparison for Moravian chroniclers of high water in that river, in the last century.

* A triangle of 2 acres, in the extreme southeast corner of the Ysselstein land, was sold to William Lynn of Saucon, in 1828, and upwards of 107 acres adjacent, to John Riegel, better known as *Herrnhuter John*, in 1829, at the rate of $45 per acre.

When Boehler and his company of Moravian refugees arrived in the Forks of Delaware from Georgia, in the spring of 1740, they experienced much kindness from the Hollander's family, all the members of which (excepting the father who deceased on the 26th of July, 1742) eventually united with the Moravians at Bethlehem.

Isaac Ysselstein left six daughters, as follows:

1. Jannetje, born in Esopus, married Philip Rudolph Haymer of Saucon, and after his decease, John Nicholas Schaeffer of Bethlehem. She died at Nazareth.

2. Cornelia, born 25th January, 1731, in Clavcrack, Albany county, married Lewis Huebner of Bethlehem, potter, 4th October, 1757,—died at that place 3d June, 1775. The late Abraham Huebner, M. D., was a grandson.

3. Eleonora, born 21st June, 1733, in Marbletown, married Abraham Andress of Bethlehem, last from Frederic township, Philadelphia county, wheelwright, 29th July, 1757,—died at Bethlehem, 14th September, 1804.

4. Beata, born in Marbletown, 10th May, 1737, married Anthony Smith of Bethlehem, tinsmith, 14th October, 1766,—died at that place, 6th July, 1814.

5. Sarah, born in Saucon township, 27th January, 1740,—died at Bethlehem, 6 January, 1785.

6. Rachel, born in Saucon township, 8th June, 1741, married Conrad Gerhardt of Philadelphia, in 1768,—died in that city, 31st May, 1801. The late Dr. William W. Gerhardt of Philadelphia, "distinguished as an author and a practitioner in medical science," the late Benjamin Gerhardt and Mrs. Henry Du Pont were her grandchildren.

Rachel, Isaac Ysselstein's widow, married Abraham Boemper of Bethlehem, silversmith, in July of 1748. She died at that place, 1st March, 1769.

Isaac Ysselstein, it was stated above, died in the night of 26th July, 1742. His remains were interred on his farm next day, Peter Boehler, of Bethlehem, conducting the services at the grave. Twenty years ago a pile of gray stones in among the second growth of timber marked the spot. Since then, however, a busy town, with giant mills and shops has sprung up on the site of the Ysselstein Farm, obliterating in its growth all landmarks of the olden times,—and so it has come to pass that no one knows precisely where the Hollander lies; but it is said that day after day, and night after night, the ceaseless rolling of iron wheels shakes his mouldering bones and dust, as the ponderous trains sweep impetuously over the place of his sepulture.

2.

TREATING OF THE OLD GRAVE-YARD ON THE HILL, ON THE SOUTH SIDE OF THE LEHIGH, NEAR THE INTERSECTION OF SECOND AND OTTAWA STREETS.

The following interments made in this place of burial, in the interval berween January of 1747 and October of 1763, are extracted from official records.

1. Margaret, m. n. Lindemann, born near Worms in the Palatinate, wife of Frederic Hartmann, died 12th January, 1747, at the Bethlehem Inn.

2. Margaret, daughter of Peter and Ann Hoffmann of Macungy, died 21st August, 1747.

3. John Fahs of Saucon township, deceased 7th September, 1747.

4. Adam, infant son of Peter and Ann Hoffmann of Macungy, died 26th October, 1747.

5. Henry, alias *Notematwemat* (signifying in the Unami Delaware, "one can't hold great mountains"), a Delaware Indian, born at "the time when corn was being hoed a second time" in 1731, in an Indian town in West Jersey, opposite Hunter's Settlement, now Lower Mount Bethel. Baptized at Bethlehem in January of 1749, died 13th February, 1752.

6. Henry, a Delaware, infant son of the above, died 24th February, 1752.

7. Luke, a Delaware, deceased 14th January, 1757.

8. Abraham, a Delaware, son of Jonathan and Verona of the Gnadenhutten Mission, died 2d July, 1757.

9. William Tatamy, a son of Moses Tatamy (interpreter to David Brainerd during his residence in the Forks of Delaware), a Delaware, attached to the Presbyterian Church in Northampton County,—died 9th August, 1757, in the house of John Jones of

Bethlehem township, from the effects of a gunshot wound received at the hands of a white boy in the Craig Settlement, while on his way with Tadeuskundt's Indians from Fort Allen to Easton to a treaty.

10. Johanna, a Delaware from Lechawachneck (Pittston), one of Tadeuskundt's company, died 9th August, 1757, immediately after baptism, administered on the Simpson Tract by Rev. Jacob Schmick.

11. Lazara, a Delaware, died 3d September, 1757.

12. Christiana, a Delaware, infant daughter of Nathaniel and Priscilla, deceased 28th November, 1757.

13. A Delaware boy aged seven years, died 3d February, 1758.

14. Justina, a Delaware, died 22d March, 1759.

15. —— Froneck, a white boy, whose body was recovered from the river, he having eight days previous to his interment, while fording the Lehigh with his father, six miles above Bethlehem, fallen from their horse and drowned. Interred 2d June, 1760.

16. Andrew Morrison, born in New England, but an inhabitant of Virginia, who after having lain ill at The Crown for four weeks, died 31st March, 1761.

17. Capt. Jacob Wetherhold of the Province Service, commissioned a Lieutenant in Major Parson's town-guard, 20th December, 1755. Mortally wounded in the affair at John Stenton's in Allen township, on the 8th October, 1763. Died at The Crown 9th October, 1763.

3.

TREATING OF INDIAN NAMES OCCURRENT IN THE FOREGOING HISTORY.

Hockendauqua, corrupted from *hack-i-un-doch-wen* (compounded of *hacki,* land, *un-doch-wen,* to come for some purpose) and signifying, *searching for land.* Mr. Heckewelder is of opinion that this word was used by the Delawares with allusion to the first advent of the whites to their settlement on the Hockendauqua, for the purpose of prospecting for or selecting lands along that creek.

Le-chau-wiëch-ink, Le-chau-wêk-ink or *Le-chau-wêk-i* (compounded of *Le-chau-wiech-en,* the fork of a road and *ink,* the local suffix) signifying *at the place of the forks of the road, where there is a fork of the road,* was the name given by the Delawares to the so-called West Branch of their national river, because, says Heckewelder, at a point on its left bank below Bethlehem a number of trails *forked off* from the great highway of travel, by which they were wont to come northward from their seats in the lower portions of the Province. *Le-chau-wĕk-i* was shortened by the German settlers into *Lĕ-cha,* a name in current use at the present day among descendants of the old Moravians at Bethlehem.

Le-chau-wa-quot, a sapling with a fork, *Le-chau-han-ne,* the fork of a stream, *Lal-chau-uch-si-ta-ja,* the forks of the toes, and *Lal-chau-wu-lin-scha-ja,* the forks of the fingers, are other words, all carrying in them the common idea of divergence or *forking.*

The earliest recorded notices of this river date back to 1701. In that year the Proprietary and Governor informed his Council, "that a young Swede arriving from *Lechay* brought intelligence that some young men on going out to hunt at *Lechay* heard the frequent reports of fire-arms, which made them suspect that the Senecas were coming down among them." Again—"the Governor censured a Marylander for endeavoring to settle a trade with the Indians on *Lechay,* despite a law prohibiting non-residents to trade with Indians in this Province." And, finally—"the Governor ordered *Op-pe-mĕ-ny-hook,* the chief of the Indians on *Lechay,* to be sent for to consult with him about passing a law prohibiting all use of rum to the Indians of his nation."

Macungy, corrupted from *Machk-un-tschi* signifying *the feeding place of bears. Machk,* a bear—*Mach-qui-ge-u,* plenty of bears. *Mach-quik,* there are plenty of bears. As early as 1735, we meet with this name written *Macaunsie* and *Macqueunsie.*

Mauch Chunk, corrupted from *Mach-wach-tschunk* (compounded of *Machk,* bear, *wach-tschu* mountain, and *ink* the local suffix) signifying, *where bear mountain is, or the place of bear mountain.*

Minisink, corrupted from *Min-sink* (compounded of *Minsi* and *ink* the local suffix) signifying, *at the place of the Minsis, where there are Minsis.*

Monacasy, corrupted from *Me-na-gas-si* or *Me-na-kĕs-si,* signifying *a stream with great bends, a crooked stream.* Descendants of the old Moravians at Bethlehem, rightly shorten the word into *Me-na-kes.*

The Delawares called the site of Bethlehem, *Me-na-gach-sink,* i. e., *at the place of the crooked stream.*

Saucon, corrupted from *sak-unk* (compounded of *sa-ku-wit,* the mouth of a creek, and *ink,* the local suffix) and signifying *at the place of the creek's outlet,* or, *where the creek debouches.* The most important of the various points in their country designated *Saucon* by the Delawares, was the outlet of the Big Beaver. The abundance of Indian relics taken from the flats about Shimersville, warrants the conjecture that a populous Indian town had once occupied its site. When alluding to it, the Indians in accordance with the genius of their language, would simply say, *sakunk,* i. e., "the town, *at the place where the creek has its outlet.*

Shamokin, corrupted from *shach-a-mĕk-ink* (compounded of *shach-a-meek,* an eel, and *ink* the local suffix) and signifying, *at the place of eels.*

Susquehanna, written in early times *sasquehanna,* corrupted from *Que-ni-schach-ach-gek-han-ne* (compounded of *quin,* long, *shach-ach-ki,* straight, and *han-ne,* stream), the name by which the Delawares originally designated the reach of the West Branch westward from the Muncy creek (in this reach stood the Delaware town of Queni-schachachki, perhaps, on the site of Linden)—then the West Branch, and finally the main stream of the great river. The Five Nation Indians, however, called the West Branch and its valley, *Otzinachson,* i. e., *the Demon's Den,* from a cave in the mountains on its right shore just above Shamokin. *Otzinachson* is corrupted variously, in old records thus, *Zinachson, Quimachson, Oxenaxa* and *Chenasky.*

Tioga, corrupted from *Ti-a-o-ga,* an Iroquois word, signifying *a gate,* or *place of entrance,* the name given by the Six Nation Indians to the neck of land in the forks of the Tioga and the North Branch, which, at one time, was the only authorized point of entrance into their country for the traveller coming northward from the country of the Delawares.

Tulpehocken, corrupted from *Tul-pe-wi-hack-i* (compounded of *tul-pe,* a turtle, and *hack-i* land) signifying *the land of turtles.* This was the Delaware name of the valley of the Tulpehocken, as well as of an old Indian town, said to have occupied the site of Womelsdorf in Berks county.

4.

TREATING OF THE FIRST BRIDGE OVER THE LEHIGH AT BETHLEHEM, AND OF "THE BIG SPRING."

The following "Song of the Bridge," was written by the Rev. Jacob Van Vleck, the second Principal of the Young Ladies Seminary at Bethlehem, for the amusement of his son the late Rt. Rev. William Henry Van Vleck, then (1794) in the fourth year of his age. But while the fond parent has playfully put words of childish wonderment into the mouth of the little boy, he has also made him speak history, which may warrant the insertion here in its entirety of

DAS BRUECKENLIED.

Wenn ich mir den Brueckenbau
In dem Lecha Strom beschau,
O! so denk ich—das ist schœn,
Bald kann man hinueber gehn.
Doch ich wag es eher nicht
Bis ich weiss dass sie nicht bricht.

Stark seh'n zwar die Balken aus
Fuer so eine kleine Maus,
Doch nach meiner Hasenart,
Die sich manchmal offenbar't
Mœcht ich doch zuvœrderst seh'n,
Einen Wagen drueber gehn.

Dann lauf ich getrost drauf hin,
Zu der Mammy Schindlerin,
Wenn sie nehmlich drueben bleibt,
Und noch laenger Wirthschaft treibt.
Sie ist doch schon alt und schwach,
Liebt ihr eignes Dach und Fach.

Nun, dem sey nun wie ihm will,
Henry freut sich in der Still',
Dass er als ein alter Mann
Einmal kuenftig sagen kann,
Dass in seinem vierten Jahr
Diese Brueck' gebauet war.

Des Baumeister's Nam' war *Trucks*—
Da die Lecha stark anwuchs
Bald im Anfang, und's Geruest
Weggeworfen worden ist,
Hat er's dauerhaft gemacht,
Und das Werk zu Stand' gebracht.

Sein Mitmeister's Nam' hiess *Hunt*,
Der sein *Bus'ness* gut verstund—
Woodring half auch fleissig dran,
Und noch mancher starker Mann;
Henry sah derweil in Ruh
Oft dem Bau der Bruecke zu.

Nun wenn starke Wasserfluth
Dieser Brueck' nicht Schaden thut,
Und wenn starker Eisgang nicht
Krachend sie in Stuecke bricht—
O! so hat's nicht leicht Gefahr
Diese Brueck' steht hundert Jahr!

The construction of the Lehigh Valley Railroad on the Simpson Tract, involved, among the rest, the ruin of what forty years ago was a favorite resort on the banks of the Lehigh for coffee and tea parties, its central point being a never-failing spring well guarded by masonry, and accessible by a flight of stone steps which led you down to the cool recesses of the grateful pool. The high bank at this point (half way between the site of the Ferry and the Island) had been cut away so as to allow of placing tables and benches. These improvements were made about 1812, when patriotism at Bethlehem ran high and demanded room for public demonstration; and the little amphitheatre being overarched by forest trees, was a charming spot on a summer's afternoon or evening. It was customary for the young men of Bethlehem on every Whit-Monday, early in the morning, to join together in repairing the precincts of this common resort, on the opening of the season of the year in which it would again be sought by the families of the town. Its grounds included the hillside from the bridge to the Island. These were threaded by numerous pathways that lead you through laurels and under noble old trees, over by far the most romantic stretch of sylvan wilderness along the Lehigh at Bethlehem. The "Big Spring" is noted down on Reuter's draft of 1757, about forty rods due north from the grave-yard on the Simpson Tract.

5.

TREATING OF THE DISMEMBERMENT OF THE OLD MORAVIAN FARMS LYING ON THE SOUTH BANK OF THE LEHIGH IN GENERAL, AND OF THAT OF THE SIMPSON TRACT IN PARTICULAR.

When, in the early winter of 1844, the Moravians, relinquishing their hereditary policy which was one of extreme exclusiveness, began to dispose of real estate in Bethlehem in fee, an important step was taken toward inviting settlement and enterprise to that town and its vicinity.

In 1847 Chas. A. Luckenbach of Bethlehem purchased of the Moravian Society its four farms lying south of the Lehigh river within Lower Saucon and Salisbury townships, to wit: "The Hoffert Farm," "The Fuehrer Farm," "The Jacobi Farm," and "The Luckenbach Farm." They were conveyed to him by Philip H. Goepp, agent, by indentures bearing date of 1st April 1848, and sold at the rate of $75 per acre. This great sale included almost the entire Simpson Tract, the upper Ysselstein tract, and portions of the Hartman, the Vollert, the Schaus, the Boerstler and the Penn tracts, lying west and south of the first two mentioned, and contained 519 acres and 129 perches,—excepting a few acres, all under cultivation.

Prior to this sale, however,—viz.: in April of 1845, 1 acre and 151 perches of the Simpson Tract, adjoining the Philadelphia stage-road on the west near the covered bridge (on it stood the old ferry-house), had been sold to Daniel Desh of Saucon township. This was the first blow aimed at its integrity. Furthermore, in April of 1846, 2 acres and 10 perches of mountain land, cut by the west line of the historic tract, were sold to Francis H. Oppelt of Bethlehem, whose "Lehigh Mountain Springs Water Cure," was then in course of erection;—and about the same time, Daniel Desh purchased three-quarters of an acre (the so-called "Walter Lot" *) situate on the Allentown road, a few rods southwest from the site of the old ferry.

---

* The log-house standing next to the Anthracite Building, as you pass up Lehigh street, was built about 1807, and was occupied by Joseph Till. Mr. Till was a shoemaker, and there are

By indentures bearing date of 1st April 1848, Chas. A. Luckenbach conveyed to Chas. C. Tombler of Bethlehem, 107 acres and 6 perches, to L. Oliver Tombler, of the same place, 32 acres and 21 perches, and to Francis H. Oppelt, 6 acres and 105 perches (land all lying west of the Emmaus road), at from $70 to $80 per acre—thus disposing of the Hoffert Farm in its entirety. Seventy acres more or less of this farm were Simpson land.

Again, by indenture bearing date of the aforementioned day of April, Chas. A. Luckenbach conveyed to Daniel Desh the Fuehrer Farm in its entirety (it contained 98 acres and 158 perches) at the rate of $95 per acre. Seventy-five acres more or less of this farm were Simpson land.

Finally, by indenture bearing date of 1st April 1848, Chas. A. Luckenbach conveyed to Joseph Hess of Lower Saucon, the Jacobi Farm (it contained 103 acres and 83 perches) in its entirety, at the rate of $80 per acre. Seventy acres, more or less of this farm, were Simpson land. Its ancient house and barns stand to the present day at the corner of Brodhead avenue and Fourth street in the borough of South Bethlehem, the only memorials remaining to indicate that agricultural pursuits had occupied the attention of some former dwellers on the site of that busy town.

The fourth and largest of these farms (it contained 160 acres more or less, 30 of which were Simpson land) was retained by the purchaser for several years, being farmed by tenants or leased. In 1849 Mr. Luckenbach supplanted the old farm-house by a brick dwelling, the same, which at present contains the office of C. C. Tombler, station agent, and offices in the freight department of the Lehigh Valley Railroad Company.

To return to the Hoffert Farm. By indenture bearing date of 7th August 1850, L. Oliver Tombler conveyed to Daniel C. Freytag of Bethlehem, 22 acres and 21 perches of his portion of the old farm, and in April of 1851, the remaining 10 acres to Augustus Fiot, of Philadelphia. Meanwhile, Mr. Fiot had purchased of Chas. C. Tombler, the 107 acres described above, the conveyance

old residents of Bethlehem, who relate that it was incumbent upon him, when they were boys, to repair the foot-gear of the rising generation, and that hence he was wont to inveigh impetuously against their pastime of hunting rabbits in the wild adjacents of the Hoffert Farm, denouncing the sport as destructive of shoe leather, and, as crowding his bench inconveniently with work.

being made by indenture dated 2d December 1850. Two years prior to this sale however Mr. Tombler had erected a stone dwelling, a few rods south from the old farm-house, which dwelling Mr. Fiot subsequently enlarged. The latter also added 29 acres and 49 perches of woodland (a portion of the Vollert tract) to his estate, improved and beautified the farm and grounds, and named his seat Fontainebleau (now Bishopthorpe). Mr. Freyteg, in April of 1856, sold his place (he had erected a dwelling on the premises in 1851, at present the residence of Tinsley Jeter) to Mrs. Malvina F. Wheeler of Mauch Chunk. She, in November of 1860, conveyed the property to Tinsley Jeter, formerly of Amelia County, Virginia, but late of Philadelphia. Augustus Fiot died in April of 1866, devising his estate to Julius Fiot, who, by indenture bearing date the 23d July, 1869, conveyed to Tinsley Jeter what lands he had become possessed of at Bethlehem, in their entirety. Thus, excepting a few acres, the old Hoffert Farm, passed into the hands of Mr. Jeter. On his entering into possession of the Fiot estate (this was in 1866) he continued the town-plot that had been projected on the Fuehrer Farm by Messrs. Hacker and Shipley, thereby throwing into the market, sites for suburban residences, which overlook one of the most charming landscapes in the Lehigh Valley. The day is not far distant, when all vestiges of the old Moravian mountain-farm will have disappeared, and its place be occupied by a beautiful town.*

To return to the Fuehrer Farm. By indenture bearing date of 20th May 1854, Daniel Desh conveyed to Rudolphus Kent of Philadelphia this farm in its entirety and his prior purchase of Simpson land, together amounting to 101 acres and 109 perches at $200 per acre. Mr. Kent, hereupon, sold a parcel of 10 acres of the above (and with it the old Crown Inn), to the North Pennsylvania Railroad Company, at the rate of $1,000 per acre,—and extended the town-plot of Wetherill (which had been projected on the Luckenbach Farm) westward of the Philadelphia stage-road to the extreme limits of the Fuehrer Farm. Lots in this extension

* In selecting names for the streets in his extreme westerly extension of South Bethlehem, Mr. Jeter has among others very appropriately adopted those of the tenants of the old farm and of the first settlers on adjacent tracts, to wit: Weygand, Kieffer, Clewell, Hoffert, Tombler and Ostrom.

(subsequently, after having been entirely changed as to its streets by Messrs. Hacker and Shipley,* called Fountain Hill, Golden Hill or Episcopal Hill, according as men followed the bent of their humor), offering eligible sites for building, found ready purchasers. Robt. H. Sayre, the Superintendent and Engineer of the Lehigh Valley Railroad, built his residence (it was the first on the hill) in 1857 and 58—Wm. H. Sayre, Jr., built in 1862—John Smylie, Jr., in 1863—Elisha P. Wilbur in 1863 and 64—Dr. F. A. Martin in 1864—H. S. Goodwin in 1867, and Dr. G. B. Linderman in 1870. This was the beginning of the town of suburban residences which crowns the high land of the old Fuehrer Farm.

In the summer of 1852, Mr. Luckenbach projected a town-plot in the very heart of his farm, its west end invading the Simpson Tract. It was named Augusta, and was the origin of the present borough of South Bethlehem. Levin C. Peisert of Bethlehem took up the first building lot, in the new town,—a lot immediately east of the New Street Bridge, fronting 40 feet on the track of the Lehigh Valley Railroad, and running south 176 feet to an alley. It was deeded to him in the following year,—the consideration money being $200. Borhek and Knauss commenced work on three double frame dwellings, situate on Augusta street, on the 31st October, 1853. These were the first residences erected in the town.

Having disposed of sundry parcels of the old farm to diverse purchasers—to wit: a plot of four acres to the Pennsylvania and Lehigh Zinc Company, the same quantity to Samuel Wetherill, town-lots to Borhek and Knauss, Wm. Th. Roepper and Michael Gorman,—and 35 acres in several pieces to Asa Packer, of Mauch Chunk, for the use of the Lehigh Valley Railroad, Mr. Luckenbach, by indenture bearing date of 24th of May, 1854, conveyed the remainder of the old farm, viz.: 97 acres and 141 perches, to Chas. W. Rauch and Ambrose H. Rauch of Bethlehem.

In the summer of 1854, Charles Brodhead of Bethlehem, who held the Jacobi Farm of 103 acres and 83 perches by agreement with Joseph Hess, and the above described remainder of the Luckenbach Farm by agreement with the Messrs. Rauch, enlarged the

* Messrs. Hacker and Shipley adopted besides Lehigh, the names of Lennape, Third, Huron, Dacotah, Seminole, Pawnee, Cherokee, Ottawa, Seneca, Chippewa, Delaware and Uncas in designating the streets and avenues of their town.

plan of Augusta, and changed its name into Wetherill, in honor of the late John Price Wetherill, of Philadelphia, manufacturer. The Secretary of War, at this time, recommending the erection of National Foundries at different points in the country, a strong effort was made by the late the Honorable Richard Brodhead, to have one located in the town of Wetherill. But Government failed to act upon the Secretary's recommendation.

By indenture, bearing date of 31st March, 1855, Joseph Hess, conveyed to Charles Brodhead, the Jacobi Farm at the rate of $200 per acre. Excepting a parcel of seven acres donated by Mr. Brodhead to the Lehigh University, this farm has been cut up into lots and incorporated with the present borough of South Bethlehem. Allusion has been made to the old farm-house and barns, that survive its wreck.

In April of 1855, the remainder of the Luckenbach Farm (to wit: 97 acres and 141 perches) reverting to Chas. W. Rauch and Ambrose H. Rauch, these disposed of sundry parcels of the same as follows: to Thomas Andrews of New York, 8 acres (the site of the mammoth rolling-mill in course of erection at this writing), to the North Pennsylvania Railroad Company about 4 acres along the dividing line of the Luckenbach and Jacobi Farms, and to the Lehigh Valley Railroad Company a strip lying north of and contiguous to Andrews' lots. At the same time Charles W. Rauch retained 2 acres of the tract, situate in the extreme southwest corner of the farm. Hereupon, by indenture bearing date of 1st April 1858, the Messrs. Rauch conveyed to A. Wolle & Co. of Bethlehem, the remainder of their original purchase, viz.: 81 acres at the rate of $250 per acre. A portion of these were subsequently sold to the Bethlehem Rolling Mills and Iron Company, the remainder continuing a part of the town of Wetherill, or Bethlehem South, as the place was called in the interval between 1858 and 1865.

Thus the old Moravian farms were gradually dismembered, and the scenes of agricultural pursuits in the olden time, were transformed into scenes of modern enterprise, on which capital and labor are active in achieving marvellous triumphs in various departments of human industry.

Finally, it may interest some reader to know, that according to a "Map of the Bethlehem Tract showing the landsales from 1771 to

1854," drawn by Wm. Th. Roepper, the Simpson tract was divided among and held by the following persons, in the last mentioned year, viz.: Daniel Desh, Joseph Hess, Daniel C. Freytag, Augustus Fiot, Asa Packer, E. A. Richardson, Francis H. Oppelt, C. A. Luckenbach, C. F. Hellner, the Moravian Society at Bethlehem, and lot-holders in the town of Augusta.

6.

TREATING BRIEFLY OF THE BOROUGH OF SOUTH BETHLEHEM, OF ITS MILLS, SHOPS, CHURCHES, SCHOOLS, BRIDGES, PUBLIC INSTITUTIONS, AND WHAT ELSE BEARS UPON THE GROWTH OF THE TOWN, WHICH HAS SUPPLANTED THE OLD MORAVIAN FARMS.*

THE BETHLEHEM BRIDGE COMPANY'S BRIDGE,

near the site of the old Ferry, was built in 1841 at a cost of $7,258, and was opened for travel, 20th September of that year. This bridge is 23 feet above low-water mark, and its floor is 400 feet long by actual measurement. It is the third bridge built within 47 years on the same site.

THE LEHIGH MOUNTAIN SPRINGS WATER CURE,

established in 1846 by Dr. F. H. Oppelt. This charming sylvan retreat touches the west line of the Simpson Tract. In June of 1871 it passed into the hands of James T. Borhek of Bethlehem, by whom it was recently conveyed to Tinsley Jeter.

THE LEHIGH ZINC COMPANY.

Forty years ago, a barren outcrop of some unknown mineral substance on his farm in Upper Saucon township, Lehigh county, arrested the attention of the late Jacob Ueberroth and his neighbors, and, after having excited their inquiring curiosity (they took a wagon-load of the ore to the Mary Ann Furnace, in Berks county, where a vain attempt was made to smelt it in the cupola) was

---

* The writer desires thus to acknowledge his indebtedness to numerous gentlemen of South Bethlehem for valuab'e aid rendered him in preparing this section of the Appendix.

unheeded, and likely to be forgotten. But "the trained and observant eye of a studious man, who, with satchel and hammer was by chance passing that way on a leisure Saturday's stroll of exploration in 1845, determined the unknown mineral to be calamine, the hydro-silicate of zinc."* Mr. Wm. Th. Roepper's discovery led to a development of that almost inexhaustible deposit of rich ores of zinc,—of calamine, Smithsonite and blende, by which the extensive works of the company, whose origin is here briefly reviewed, have been supplied for almost twenty years.

The organization effected "for the purpose of mining zinc ore in the counties of Lehigh and Northampton,—of manufacturing zinc paint, metallic zinc and other articles from said ore, and of vending the same," was incorporated by an act of Legislature, May 2d, 1855, under the name of "The Pennsylvania and Lehigh Zinc Company," with a capital of $1,000,000, divided into shares of $5 each. The originators of this company were residents of New York, and its first president was Thomas Andrews of that city.

Prior to their incorporation, however, in the spring of 1853, works for the production of zinc oxide in furnaces and by a process of his own invention, were begun to be constructed by Mr. Samuel Wetherill, who had been engaged to superintend the enterprise in its various departments. The site of the company's works was purchased of C. A. Luckenbach, it being included within the original town-plot of Augusta, on the old "Luckenbach Farm." They were completed on the 12th of October of the above-mentioned year, with a capacity of 2,000 tons per annum, at a cost of $85,000—and, next day, the first zinc-white made in the United States, was pro-

* We quote from the genial address delivered by Benjamin C. Webster, the President of the Lehigh Zinc Company, on the occasion of starting the giant engine at the company's mines in Fridensville, on the 19th of January last. This is the engine which is destined to become famous as is the house that Jack built; this is the engine whose cylinder is 110 inches in diameter, whose piston rod is 10 inches in diameter with a ten-foot stroke,—this is the engine that can work "comfortably," as we are told, at 12 strokes per minute, and yet is not in the least "fussy;" the engine, each of whose four walking-beams weighs 48,000 lbs.,—twenty-six of whose pieces weigh each upwards of 7 tons, and whose entire weight, including girders, is 1,313,300 lbs.;—the engine that can lift 52,800,000 lbs., or 26,400 tons, one foot high in one minute of time with the majestic ease and consciousness of power with which an elephant lifts a straw; the engine that can raise 12,000 gallons of water per minute from a depth of 300 feet—which works day and night without rest; and whose influence is a mighty one towards transforming the subterranean haunts of Kobalt and gnome, where, from times Silurian these spirits have sported undisturbed in the ice-cold sea that noiselessly washes the shores of their crystal kingdom.

duced from calamine by the "furnace process" and "tower process" of Wetherill, in combination with the "bag process of collecting," of Richard Jones. Samuel Wetherill and Charles T. Gilbert conducted the company's works for four years, from October, 1853, to September, 1857, and in that time delivered 4,725 tons of zinc-white. The present capacity of the oxide works, which are supervised by James McMahon, is 3,000 tons per year. It should here be stated, that in the interval between 1854 and 1859, Mr. Wetherill experimented on the production of metallic zinc or spelter, at works erected by him on a four-acre lot adjoining that of the Pennsylvania and Lehigh Company—the upper end of said lot lying within the limits of the historic Simpson Tract. Here the inventor succeeded, after many expensive failures and disappointments, in producing spelter—not, however, at a cost such as to characterize his method as an economically practicable one. Hence it was abandoned.

Joseph Wharton managed the Pennsylvania and Lehigh Zinc Company's works between September of 1857, and September of 1860. In this interval its corporate title was changed by an act of Legislature, dated 16th February, 1860, into that of "The Lehigh Zinc Company," by which it continues to be known. In 1859 Mr. Wharton contracted with the company for the erection of spelter works, and for the manufacture of the metal. The works were constructed by Louis De Gée, a member of the firm of De Gée, Gernant & Co., of Ougrèe, Province of Liege, Belgium, who had been expressly imported to superintend the inception of the enterprise. This led to the importation of Belgian labor, and to the consequent introduction of a new element into the population of Bethlehem South. André Woot Detrixhe, François Lemall, and Jean Henrard, experts from the spelter and oxide works of Messrs. De Gée, Gernant & Co., arrived in June of 1859, and engaged successfully in the production of metallic zinc, the first of which was cast in July of that year. M. Detrixhe since that time has superintended this department of the company's works, including the pottery for the manufacture of retorts. There were four subsequent importations of Belgians;—in 1860, one of fifteen; in 1861, one of nine; in 1863, one of six; and in 1864, one of twenty-seven. These operatives are principally from Ougrèe, and from Ongleur, Vielle Montagne; some, however, from St. Léonard, Vielle Montagne, native of the Provinces of Liége, Luxembourg and Namour, Belgium.* They have laid aside the blue blouse and their women have exchanged the *sabot* for the American shoe; but both, by clinging to the mother tongue, are maintaining their distinctiveness as a people in the marvellous little town of many nations, for homes in which they exchanged the land of their birth.

The capacity of the Pennsylvania and Lehigh Company's spelter works, at present, is 3,600 tons per year.

In 1864 and 1865 a mill for rolling sheet-zinc was constructed under the superintendence of Alexander Trippel, who had been sent abroad to acquaint himself with the most desirable mode of producing this important commodity. The first sheet-zinc was rolled in April of 1865. The present capacity of the mill is 3,000 casks, or 1,680 tons, per year.

James Jenkins succeeded Joseph Wharton in the management of this novel branch of American industry, which although, comparatively speaking, in its infancy, already supplies one-half of the home consumption of zinc in its various forms.

Benjamin C. Webster, the fifth President of the Lehigh Zinc Company, has been acting manager of its works since September of 1863.

The annual yield of the zinc mines, which are situate in Saucon Valley, three miles and a half south by west from Bethlehem, is estimated to be 17,000 tons of ore, requiring 40,000 tons of anthracite for their reduction. Upwards of 600 operatives are employed in the various departments of the Lehigh Zinc Company's enterprise.

---

* The following is an enumeration of the Belgian metallurgists imported by the Pennsylvania and Lehigh Zinc Company: In June of 1859, Andre Woot Detrixhe, Francois Lemall, and Jean Henrard. In January of 1860, Louis Degee, Charles Barthelemy, and Ferdinand Niset. In July of 1860, Ferdinand Woot Detrixhe, Nicolas Woot Detrixhe, Philippe Vooz, Augustin Vooz, Jacques Lemall, Desire Poupier, Hubert Dubois, Isidore Wilmotte, Gilles Franket, Servais Evrard, Jean Evrard, and Francois Evrard. In May of 1861, Antoine Dessurny, Jean Bodson, Loius Mordent, Laurent De Couny, Antoine Gerard, Theodore Georis, Servais Ranson, Joseph Cambresy, and Guillaume Giltai. In May of 1863, Henri Vooz, Dieudonne Nelis, Jacques Tribolet, Pierre Waltery, Dirick Benoit, and Louis Gerard. In September of 1864, Sebastien Delfosse, Lambert Jacob, Emile Radard, Michel Massart, Piron Massart, Henri Missoten, Francois Vandevert, Arnold Classen, Jean Bawdin, Lambert Schouben, Antoine Ledoux, Francois Lalloux, Nicolas Labaloue, Lambert Barbier, Henri Philippet, Joseph Dedoyard, Guillaume Dedoyard, Joseph Beau Jean, Gustave Lignoul, Jules Vandermassen, Ferdinand Vandermassen, Frederick Vandermassen, Hippolite Vandermassen, Nicolas Dorne, Jean Frankson, Henri Chatherlain, and Joseph Legraire.

THE LEHIGH VALLEY RAILROAD.

The company which controls this now great highway of travel and traffic was organized originally under the name of "The Delaware, Lehigh, Schuylkill and Susquehanna Railroad Company," by an act of Assembly dated 21st April, 1846. A supplement to said act, under date of 7th January, 1853, changed the title of the corporation to the one by which it is at present known. The original main line of the Lehigh Valley Railroad (following the courses of the river whose name it bears for a distance of 46 miles from Mauch Chunk to Easton), was located in 1852, and constructed between 27th November of that year and the 24th September, 1855. On the last mentioned day it was delivered complete to the company by Asa Packer, who had the contract for the work, and was accepted. Prior to that date, however, viz., on the 11th of June, 1855, the road was opened for the transportation of passengers from South Easton to Allentown, two trains running daily to the latter place until the 12th of September ensuing; then it was opened to Mauch Chunck, with one train a day until the 1st of October. But the first locomotive engine that was ever driven over the Simpson Tract was the General Wall, which came up by this road to the new town of Wetherill, on the evening of the 4th of June, 1855.

The brick dwelling erected on the Luckenbach Farm in 1849, served for the first station-house at Bethlehem for the Lehigh Valley Railroad. This was superseded in 1859 by a station-house (used in common with the North Pennsylvania Railroad), built at the intersection of the two roads, near the site of the old ferry-house. This landmark, as has been stated elsewhere, was demolished, when the bed of the road was levelled, as it lay in its very track.

The present commodious station-house, built at the joint expense of the Lehigh Valley Railroad and the North Pennsylvania Railroad, in 1867 (it cost upwards of $23,000), called the Union Depot,—furnished with public rooms for the use of both roads and with separate offices for each, was occupied on the 18th of November, 1867. With its spacious platforms it covers the site of the old Crown Inn and that of its yard and garden. The historic hostelry stood near the south-east angle of the southern platform; and scarcely a rod beyond, is pointed out the track which passes over the well, at which its successive landlords drew the water which the thirsty traveller needed for qualifying his chosen beverage.

In 1864 and in 1870 additions were built to the aforementioned dwelling on the Luckenbach Farm, in which, among others, are the offices of Robert H. Sayre, General Superintendent and Chief Engineer of the Road; of William H. Sayre, Jr., the President's assistant; of H. Stanley Goodwin, Assistant General Superintendent; of H. S. Kitchell, Chief Clerk; of Calvin E. Brodhead, Principal Assistant Engineer of the Easton and Amboy Railroad Company; of George H. Daugherty, Architect of the Lehigh Valley Railroad, and of John D. Trimmer, Freight Car Agent. The Western Union Telegraph Company, Oliver A. Clewell, manager, established an office in these buildings in September of 1871.

The Lehigh Valley Railroad, in its course along the river's banks at Bethlehem, traverses four of the old Moravian tracts, to wit: the Hartman tract, the Ostrom tract, the Simpson tract, and the Ysselstein tract. Day after day, and night after night, the rolling of its trains of burden and palace-cars (upwards of seventy-five trains pass the site of the old Crown Inn, every twenty-four hours)—some laden with human freight, some with merchandise,—(some, too, for a time carried tea direct from the Celestial Empire, and in return the "great China mail" on its passage over the Atlantic to the Golden Gate, thence to be conveyed across the great Pacific Sea)—but most with anthracite;—these, endless trains, drawn by giant ten-wheeled engines,—together with the calls of shrill or booming whistles, are re-echoed by the mountain over the little valley which their irresistible influences have so wonderfully changed.

The total amount of anthracite coal transported over the main line and branches of this road for the fiscal year ending 30th November, 1871, was 2,889,074 tons. During the same period, there were transported 867,721 passengers, equal to 13,412,064 carried one mile, and 1,573,746 tons of miscellaneous freight, equal to 53,165,973 tons carried one mile.

THE NORTH PENNSYLVANIA RAILROAD.

The company which constructed this important link in the great chain of Pennsylvania's railroads, by which, too, Bethlehem has been brought within two hours from Philadelphia, was incorporated by an

Act of Legislature dated 8th April, 1852, under the name of The Philadelphia, Easton and Water-Gap Railroad Company. Ground was first broken on the Tunnel Section at Landis' Ridge on the 16th of June, 1853. On the 3d of October of that year, the corporate title of the company was changed into the one it bears at present. The first passenger train ran from Philadelphia to the Freemansburg station, on the Lehigh Valley Railroad (the then northern terminus of the road), on the 1st of January, 1857. On the 1st of July of the same year, the track was closed at Iron Hill (Irish's stone quarry), and a construction train was run through to the Bethlehem station. On the 8th of July the passenger trains were taken off the Freemansburg branch, and began to run regularly over the main line to and from Bethlehem. This marked the opening of the road. The right of way over the old Moravian Farms and ground for the buildings requisite at its northern terminus, were purchased for the company by its commissioner, Rudolphus Kent—as has been stated elsewhere. The first station-house was held in common with the Lehigh Valley Railroad; and stood in the intersection of the two roads, near the site of the old Ferry House. This was superseded by the Union Depot, which was erected at the joint expense of the two roads, and was occupied on the 18th November, 1867. Besides public rooms for the use of both roads, it contains the office of H. P. Hammann, the Company's General Agent at Bethlehem, and those of other officials under his supervision.

The first round-house of the North Pennsylvania Railroad at Bethlehem, was built in 1857. This was superseded in 1870 by a more capacious one with stalls for fifteen engines. It stands literally *below* where was the site of the "Crown Farm" orchard, it having been necessary to dig away the hill on which the ancient apple trees stood, to locate the building on a level with the bed of the railroad. The Freight Depot, a few rods east by south from the station on the Luckenbach Farm, was completed in 1870. It is built of brick, 100 feet by 30 feet, roofed with slate, with a shed 70 feet by 25 feet, attached,—the entire building being surrounded by platforms. Its cost was $8,000.

The track of the North Pennsylvania Railroad soon after crossing the "old King's Road, from the Bethlehem Mill to Irish's stone quarry," passes by or over Isaac Ysselstein's grave, opposite the head of Ysselstein Island,—and on the west side of the run that flows under its bed, follows the old dividing line of the Luckenbach and Jacobi Farms, till within the Simpson Tract. In pursuing this course thence in a northwesterly direction, it passes over the very site of the old Crown Inn, and then near that of the Ferry House, beyond which it joins the Lehigh Valley Railroad. To be more precise. The first or lowest track of the North Pennsylvania Railroad was located so as to cut the southwest corner of The Crown—and hence the site of the historic hostelry is almost entirely covered by a portion of the south platform of the Union Depot.

Six passenger trains pass over the line of this road daily, Sundays excepted. They set out from the very spot on which Samuel Powell and his successors dispensed hospitality in the olden time. They land their human freight on the same spot; and such has been the improvement in travel, since the days of John Koppel, and Klein's stage-wagon, that passenger-train No. 6 (commonly called the Buffalo express), which leaves the Bethlehem station at 8.40 P. M., makes the run of 54 miles to Philadelphia, in one hour and fifty minutes.

For the fiscal year ending 31st October, 1871, there were transported over this road 829,651 passengers, equal to 15,305,399 carried one mile,—227,440 tons coal, 359,219 tons of miscellaneous freight, 46,889 tons of pig iron, 333,345 bushels of lime, and 2,498,438 gallons of milk,—thus, far exceeding the capacity of Koppel's "slow and sure" freight line of the days of yore. Now the last-mentioned item of transportation suggested the poetical name of Galaxy or Milky Way, by which this road is also not unknown.

THE FOUNDRY AND MACHINE SHOP,

below the offices of the Lehigh Valley Railroad, on the site of the yard of the Luckenbach Farm, was established by Abbott and Cortright in 1857.

THE BETHLEHEM IRON COMPANY AND THEIR WORKS ON THE UPPER YSSELSTEIN TRACT.

Early in the month of March, 1857, the senior partner of the firm of A. Wolle & Co., of Bethlehem, merchants, desirous of making an effort in a new direction for enlarging the business sphere of his native place, so highly favored by its situation in a region of country whose mineral wealth was beginning to be developed, and by its position on the highways of travel, proposed to his partners the erection of works for the production and manufacture of iron. The proposal meeting with their approbation, Mr. Wolle, before the expiration of four weeks, had procured a charter for the projected company, styled in that instrument, which was dated 8th April, 1857, "The Saucona Iron Company."

The summer and early autumn of the afore-mentioned year were spent in soliciting stock subscription, and in exploring the neighborhood for ore, in both of which preliminary steps, encouraging progress was being made, when the financial crisis which followed the suspension of The Ohio Life Insurance and Trust Company, paralyzed the infant enterprise, and its further prosecution was indefinitely postponed. Up to this time it had been fostered mainly by the firm of A. Wolle & Co., Charles W. Rauch and Charles Brodhead, all of Bethlehem, and remained an unorganized body corporate.

Two years of apparent inactivity followed this postponement. These, however, proved of incalculable benefit to the dormant enterprise, as meanwhile numerous applications for the construction and management of the proposed works coming in from various quarters, an opportunity was afforded the company of satisfactorily canvassing the merits of the applicants. Charles B. Daniel, of Bethlehem, and Robert H. Sayre, of the Lehigh Valley Railroad, becoming associated with the project, and the corporate title of the company having been changed at the suggestion of Charles Brodhead (he taking the ground that a Rolling Mill would furnish occupation for more labor than a blast furnace), by an act of Legislature, dated 31st March, 1757, into that of "The Bethlehem Rolling Mills and Iron Company;"—it was now vigorously prosecuted, and an important step towards its successful achievement was taken, by securing the services of John Fritz, of Johnstown, Cambria county, a master in his profession, to superintend the construction of the works, and then the production and manufacture of the metal.

On the 14th of June, 1860, the new company elected its first Board of Directors, and on the 7th of July ensuing, organized with the following officers, viz.:

President.—Alfred Hunt, Philadelphia.

Directors.—Augustus Wolle, Bethlehem; Asa Packer, Mauch Chunk; John Taylor Johnston, of the New Jersey Central Railroad; John Knecht, Shimersville; Edward Roberts, Philadelphia; Charles B. Daniel, Bethlehem; Charles W. Rauch, Bethlehem.

Secretary and Treasurer.—Charles B. Daniel.

On the 16th day of July, ground was broken for a furnace (now called Furnace No. 1), on a parcel of eleven acres of ground lying between the track of the Lehigh Valley Railroad and the old Hellertown road; said parcel having been purchased of Abbott, Cortright & Co., at $300 per acre,—the company at the same time purchasing of A. Wolle & Co., six acres of land situate between the aforesaid road and the Lehigh river, at the rate of $150 per acre. Work at this furnace was progressing slowly, when, in the spring of 1861, the country found itself on the eve of a civil war. A critical period in the history of the company now ensued. There followed six months of almost total inactivity, and but for the strenuous efforts of A. Wolle and Charles W. Rauch, in all probability the enterprise would have been entirely suspended for a time.

By an act of Assembly dated 1st May, 1861, the company's corporate title was changed into that of "The Bethlehem Iron Company."

Meanwhile work at the furnaces was progressing nominally only, until in the autumn of 1862, when it was resumed with vigor. The stack (115 feet boshes and 63 feet high) was completed by the close of the year, and on Sunday, 4th of January, 1863, Mr. Jedediah Weiss, of Bethlehem, fired the blast, and next day Miss Kate Powell, of Philadelphia, put on the blast. The first iron made by the Bethlehem Iron Company (it was smelted from a mixture of brown hematite from the Saucon Valley, and magnetic oxide from Morris county, New Jersey) was drawn on the 6th of January, 1863. This furnance continued in blast for thirty-four weeks, and was then blown out for slight repairs. Having been put in blast a second time on the 24th of January, 1864, it continued in that condition for three hundred and sixty-three successive weeks, producing in that time 63,007 tons of pig metal,—a record which is perhaps without parallel in the annals of metallurgy.

Meanwhile a rolling mill had been in course of construction since April of 1861. The first iron for rolling was puddled 27th of July,

1863, and the first rails were rolled 26th of September, 1863. This mill contains 4 engines, 14 double puddling furnaces, 9 heating furnaces and 3 trains of rolls, viz., one 21-inch rail train, one 12-inch merchant train, and one 21-inch puddle train. The capacity of these works at present is from 20,000 to 22,000 tons of railroad iron. The first heavy contract for rails was one of 2,000 tons, made with the New Jersey Central Railroad, in 1864, said amount of rails being furnished at $62.50 per ton, one-half, however, being delivered when the market ruled from $100 to $125 per ton.

Furnace No. 2 (15 feet boshes, 45 feet high), was commenced to be constructed in May of 1864. First blast fired 27th of March, 1867. Blast put on 28th of March, 1867. First iron drawn 30th of March, 1867.

In September of 1868 the Bethlehem Iron Company succeeded in merging into its own, the interests of the Northampton Iron Company, an adjacent enterprise, whose works were then in course of construction. Thereby the former strengthened its own position, besides acquiring upwards of 80 acres of valuable real estate, contiguous to its works, and also leases of iron beds at different points, held by the latter.

Furnace No. 3 (14 feet boshes, 50 feet high), until the time of the merger, called "The Northampton Furnace," was put in blast in December of 1868. First iron drawn 18th December, 1868.

The combined capacity of these three furnaces is about 30,000 tons of pig metal per annum, most of which is manufactured in the company's rolling mill.

At a meeting of the stockholders, held 28th of July, 1868, it was resolved to approve of the late suggestion of the Board of Directors to engage in the manufacture of steel rails, and that "the Superintendent take measures to construct works suitable for the manufacture of such rails without delay." Action on this resolution was at once taken, and, in September following, the construction of the Cyclopean mills, now erecting on what is known as the Andrews lot, was commenced. A machine shop (dimensions 234 feet by 64 feet), built in 1865, and furnished with the most approved appliances, and a foundry (dimensions 107 feet by 64 feet), built in 1868, enable the company to build or make the engines, pumps, rolls and whatever else is requisite for the complete equipment of the new mills, and also to keep their extensive works in repair with their own manufactures.

Rolling mill No. 2, of the Bethlehem Iron Company, built in the shape of a Greek cross, has an extreme length of 931 feet, and covers an area of 164,391 square feet, *i. e.*, upwards of 4.6 acres of ground. This colossal structure is covered with a slate roof (the slate is from the Chapman quarry), resting upon grooved arches of cast iron, without supporters, presenting in the interior an elegance of design and construction, which, perhaps, is the first point to strike the beholder's eye, as he enters its spacious aisles.

The great train for rolling steel-rails will consist of one 24, and one 26-inch roll, with a condensing-engine at each end (one, with 48-inch diameter cylinder and 46 inch stroke, the other with 56-inch diameter cylinder and 48 inch stroke)—measuring 124 feet 9 inches from center to center of the engines—making, it is thought, the largest continuous train in the world. The blooming-train of 31 inches, is run by an engine of its own. The probabilities are, that additional trains of rolls, to wit: one 9 inch, one 14 inch, and one 18 inch, will be added. The mill will also contain four sets of saws with double engine for each set, a double blowing engine for the Bessemer works, two 5-ton Bessemer converters, with a capacity of 100 tons of steel per day—a cupola engine, and a number of Sieman's Regenerative Gas Furnaces for heating purposes.

The Bethlehem Iron Company's works, at the present time consume annually 70,000 tons of Pennsylvania hematite and New Jersey magnetic oxide, and from 70,000 to 75,000 tons of coal. Upwards of 800 men are employed in its magnificent enterprise.

ST. PETER'S EVANGELICAL LUTHERAN CHURCH,

on Vine street, between Fifth street and Packer avenue. Erected in 1863. Opened for Divine Worship 26th June, 1864.

First Pastor.—Rev. A. T. Geissenhainer.

Present Pastor.—Rev. Charles J. Cooper.

There are 175 communicant members belonging to this church. Total membership 300.

CHURCH OF THE HOLY INFANCY (*Catholic*)

(Diocese of Philadelphia, Rt. Rev. James F. Wood, D. D., Bishop of Pennsylvania), on the corner of Fourth and Locust streets. Erected in 1863 and 1864. Opened for Divine Worship 24th October, 1864.

Pastor.—Rev. M. C. McEnroe.

Total membership 2,650.

A plot of two and a half acres, lying on the mountain side in the extreme southeast corner of his tract, was donated by Asa Packer to the Church of the Holy Infancy for a Cemetery. The first interment within its borders, was that of James Griffin, 22d October, 1867.

CHURCH OF THE NATIVITY (*Episcopal*),

on the south-east corner of Third street and Wyandotte street (the old Philadelphia Road). Erected in 1864 and 1865. Opened for Divine Worship 19th April, 1865.

First Pastor.—Rev. Eliphalet Nott Potter.

First Vestry.—Tinsley Jeter, South Bethlehem; William H. Sayre, South Bethlehem; Robert H. Sayre, South Bethlehem; William H. Sayre, Jr., South Bethlehem; John Smylie, Jr., South Bethlehem; Ira Cortright, Bethlehem; Asa Packer, Mauch Chunk; Solomon W. Roberts, Philadelphia.

Present Rector.—Rev. Cortlandt Whitehead.

There are 127 communicant members belonging to this church, and 75 families connected with the Parish.

THE FIRST SABBATH SCHOOL,

upon the old Moravian Tract opposite the Borough of Bethlehem, was commenced by Miss Amanda Jones of that place, on the 1st of May, 1859. Eleven children constituted the class she gathered on that day in the "District School House" of Bethlehem South. In November of 1863, this school numbered 280, and subsequently upwards of 500 children in attendance. It is still under the care of its founder and first Superintendent.

CHRISTMAS HALL,

erected in 1863 by the Moravians for a Mission Church in Bethlehem South. Opened for Divine Worship 20th November, 1864.

First Pastor.—Rev. F. F. Hagen.

This building was conveyed to the Lehigh University in 1865, and thereupon received its present name.

THE BETHLEHEM SOUTH GAS AND WATER COMPANY,

INCORPORATED APRIL, 1864,

holds the Gas Works, in the borough of South Bethlehem (on Spruce street near Third street),—constructed by B. E. Lehman in 1867, at a cost of $32,000, including the works and the distributing mains. Gas was consumed for the first time, 25th December, 1867.

Board of Directors.—President, E. P. Wilbur; Secretary and Treasurer, H. Stanley Goodwin; Superintendent, B. E. Lehman.

THE BOROUGH OF SOUTH BETHLEHEM

was incorporated under the General Borough Law at the August term, 1865, of the Court of Northampton County. The Council met for the first time 19th September, of that year.

First Burgess.—James McMahon.

Members of First Council.—Louis F. Beckel, E. P. Wilbur, James McCoy, James Purcell, David I. Yerkes.

Borough Treasurer.—Theophilus Horlacher.

Town Clerk.—William H. Bush.

High Constable.—John Kilkelly.

The limits of the borough of South Bethlehem are thus defined in the act of incorporation:

"Beginning at a point on the bank of the river Lehigh, opposite a small island" (vulgarly called Goose island) "in the line of Northampton and Lehigh Counties; thence following down the several courses of the said river, 427.45 perches to an oak opposite the head of Ysselstein's island; thence southeasterly, 30 perches to a stone in the Hellertown road; thence along the lands of Asa Packer, westerly and southwesterly, 333 perches to the northwest corner of said Asa Packer's land; thence westerly, 127.4 perches to the line of Lehigh County; and thence northeasterly, 130 perches along said line to the place of beginning."

From Messrs. Aschbach's and Hauman's authorized survey and map of the borough we learn that the following are the streets within its limits, lying east of the old Philadelphia road, to wit: Front, Second, Third, Mechanic, Fourth, Fifth, and Packer Avenue,—all running east and west; and Walnut, Chestnut (proposed), Brodhead Avenue, Vine, New, Birch, Elm, Locust, Pine, Spruce, Linden, Poplar, Oak, and Cherry,—all running north and south.

The "Zinc Mine road," deflecting from the old Philadelphia road in a northeasterly direction (now Carpenter street), crosses the western portion of the above defined plot obliquely. In March of 1869 the borough of South Bethlehem was divided into three wards, by virtue of a special act of Legislature. Its population, according to the census of 1870, was 3,550. How the people of this ambitious little town (it is a highly composite people,—a mixed population of Americans, Irish, Germans, Belgians, Welsh, English, French, Swedes, Italians, Poles and Hollanders) live,—how they buy and sell, what they eat and drink, and how they maintain the various relations incident upon their coalescence into a commonwealth, and yet preserve, each element its distinctive characteristics, may in part be inferred from an enumeration of the churches, schools, public houses, places of business and associations which they support. Of churches there are 6; of schools there are 8, including the Sabbath schools; of Societies there are 4, to wit, Knights of Pythias, numbering 200 members; the Catholic Temperance Society, numbering 230 members; the Catholic Beneficial Society, numbering 180 members; and the Sodality of the Holy Virgin, numbering 210 members. There is furthermore a cornet band and a military organization, known as "The Wilbur Guards." Of hotels there are 12, to wit, the Exchange, the Pacific, the Lehigh Valley, the Continental, the Zinc Works Hotel, the Le Pierre, the Johnstown House, the Rolling Mill House, the Sherman House, the Maréchal House, the Fountain Valley House, and the Merchants' Hotel. There are 18 licensed restaurants and saloons, 4 wholesale liquor stores, 3 justices of the peace, 6 physicans, 1 dentist, 3 bakers and confectioners, 2 jewellers, 3 blacksmiths, 6 milliners, 8 shoemakers,

2 undertakers, 1 carpet weaver, 1 leather dresser, 12 dry goods and variety stores, 2 drug stores, 3 printing offices, 2 meat markets, 3 cigar stores, 1 hardware store, 1 furniture store, 5 clothing stores, 1 shovel factory, 1 slate yard, 2 coal and lumber yards, 1 foundry and machine shop, and 1 planing mill and sash factory. Its furnaces, mills, foundries and workshops, for the production and manufacture of iron, zinc and brass, furnish employment to almost one-half of this busy people, the prosperity and rapid growth of whose town illustrate what wonders can be effected by the harmonious co-operation of capital and labor.

THE NEW STREET BRIDGE COMPANY OF BETHLEHEM, PENNSYLVANIA,

Incorporated by an act of Assembly, 3d May, 1864. Commissioners, Aaron W. Radley, John T. Levers, Richard W. Leibert, and Herman A. Doster. This company's bridge over the Lehigh river, which connects the east end of the Simpson tract with the borough of Bethlehem, was built in 1866 and 1867, at a cost of $60,000, and was opened for travel 2d of September, 1867. The structure rests upon eight piers, is thirty-six feet above low water mark, spans the track of the Lehigh and Susquehanna Railroad, the Lehigh Coal and Navigation Company's canal, the Manokasy creek, a neck of land called the Sand island, the Lehigh, and the track of the Lehigh Valley Railroad. The length of the floor of this bridge is 1046 feet by actual measurement.

First Board of Directors.—President, Charles N. Beckel; Robert H. Sayre, Elisha P. Wilbur, John J. Levers, Herman A. Doster, Robert A. Abbott.

Secretary and Treasurer.—Herman A. Doster.

Original shares were issued and sold at $50.

WATER WORKS.

In 1866 Tinsley Jeter built a small reservoir near Bishopthrope School, and laid pipes thence, through several streets, as far as the Union Depot, thus supplying Fountain Hill with mountain spring water.

THE SOUTH BETHLEHEM POST OFFICE

was established in June of 1866.

First Postmaster.—John Seem.

THE LEHIGH UNIVERSITY,

founded by the Hon. Asa Packer, Mauch Chunk, in 1865. Erected between 1866 and 1869, in the southeast corner of the Simpson Tract.

In 1865 the Hon. Asa Packer, of Mauch Chunck, announced to the Rt. Rev. William Bacon Stevens, the Bishop of Pennsylvania, his intention to appropriate $500,000 and an eligible site and grounds at South Bethlehem for an educational institution, in which he designed that opportunities should be afforded to young men of acquiring, besides a liberal education, a knowledge of those branches of science which bear directly upon the industrial pursuits concerned in developing the natural resources of the country—in schools of Civil, Mechanical and Manufacturing Engineering, of Chemistry, Architecture and Construction. This institution Mr. Packer proposed to name The Lehigh University.

Ground was broken for the main building—called Packer Hall—on 1st of July, 1866, and the exercises of the University were formally opened in Christmas Hall on the 1st of September following, in the presence of the Trustees and Faculty of the institution, the students of the first class and invited guests. Packer Hall, built in the architectural style of the Renaissance (Edward Tuckerman Potter, Architect, James Jenkins, Superintendent of Construction), of Potsdam sandstone, quarried on Ostrom's Ridge, was so far completed as to be occupied on the 4th of March, 1869.

The corps of officers of this noble Institution was constituted as follows, at the time of its opening:

Founder of the Lehigh University.—The Hon. Asa Packer, of Mauch Chunk, Pennsylvania.

Board of Trustees.—The Rt. Rev. William Bacon Stevens, D. D., LL. D., Bishop of Pennsylvania, President of the Board; the Hon. Asa Packer, Mauch Chunk; the Hon. J. W. Maynard, Easton; Robert H. Sayre, Esq., South Bethlehem; William H. Sayre, Jr., Esq., Bethlehem; Robert A. Packer, Esq., Mauch Chunk; G. B. Linderman, M. D., Mauch Chunk; John Fritz, Esq., Bethlehem; Harry E. Packer, Esq., Mauch Chunk; Joseph Harrison, Jr., Esq., Philadelphia.

Secretary.—Robert A. Packer.

Treasurer of the Fund.—Elisha P. Wilbur, Esq., South Bethlehem.

FACULTY OF THE UNIVERSITY.

President.—Henry Coppée, LL. D., Professor of History and English Literature.

Professors.—Rev. Eliphalet Nott Potter, M. A., Professor of Moral and Mental Philosophy and of Christian Evidence; Charles Mayer Wetherill, Ph. D., M. D., Professor of Chemistry (died at his residence at the University, 5th March, 1871); Edwin Wright Morgan, LL. D., Professor of Mathematics and Mechanics (died at his residence in Bethlehem, 16th April, 1869); Alfred Marshall Mayer, Ph. D., Professor of Physics and Astronomy; William Theodore Rœpper, Esq., Professor of Mineralogy and Geology and Curator of the Museum.

Instructors.—George Thomas Graham, A. B., Instructor in Latin, Greek and Mathematics; M. Henri Albert Rinck, Instructor in French and German; Stephen Paschall Sharpless, S. B., Instructor and Assistant in Chemistry.

Janitor.—Mr. Nathan Crowell Tooker.

First Class of Students (entered 1st September, 1866).—Lehman Preston Ashmead, Philadelphia; Edward C. Boutelle, Bethlehem; Richard Brodhead, South Bethlehem; William R. Butler, Mauch Chunk; George L. Cummins, Louisville, Ky.; Milton Dimmick, Mauch Chunk; J. F. Reynolds Evans, Fort Wayne, Ind.; George A. Jenkins, South Bethlehem; Henry C. Jenkins, South Bethlehem; William H. Jenkins, Wyoming; William J. Kerr, Jr., New York City; A. Nelson Lewis, Havre de Grace, Md.; Peter D. Ludwig, Tamaqua; Charles McKee, Allentown; Harry E. Packer, Mauch Chunk; William L. Paine, Wilkesbarre; Joseph M. Piollett, Towanda; Harry R. Price, Minersville; Henry B. Reed, Philadelphia; William D. Ronaldson, Philadelphia; James K. Shoemaker, Mauch Chunk; John M. Thorne, Palmyra, N. Y.; Robert P. Weston, Slatington; Charles Wetherill, Phœnixville; Russel B. Yates, Waverly, N. Y.

The first "University Day" was celebrated on the 25th of June, 1867. On the 3d of July, 1871, the Lehigh University was formally placed under the auspices of the Protestant Episcopal Church, and tuition in all the branches of instruction, was, at the wish of the founder, declared to be free.

THE MORAVIAN CHURCH IN SOUTH BETHLEHEM,

on Elm street, near Packer Avenue, erected in 1867, opened for Divine service 9th of March, 1868.

Pastor.—Rev. Henry J. Van Vleck.

Communicant members, 135; total membership, 235.

BISHOPTHROPE SCHOOL FOR GIRLS,

on the west line of the Simpson Tract, established in 1868, under the auspices of the Protestant Episcopal Church. The School was opened 5th of September of the aforementioned year.

First President.—Rt. Rev. William Bacon Stevens, D. D., LL. D., Bishop of Pennsylvania.

First Board of Trustees.—Rev. Eliphalet Nott Potter, Rector of the Church of the Nativity; Tinsley Jeter, Robert H. Sayre, William H. Sayre, Jr., James Jenkins, H. Stanley Goodwin, Dr. Henry Coppée.

First Principal.—Miss Edith L. Chase.

Present Principal.—Miss F. I. Walsh.

THE RAILROAD BRIDGE OF THE LEHIGH AND SUSQUEHANNA RAILROAD

was built by the Lehigh Coal and Navigation Company, in 1867. Its length is 438 feet by actual measurement. In the spring of 1868 the Lehigh and Susquehanna Railroad connected with the North Pennsylvania Railroad by this bridge for general business.

THE LEHIGH VALLEY BRASS WORKS,

on Front street, below the offices of the Lehigh Valley Railroad, established in 1863. B. E. Lehman, proprietor.

THE PENROSE SCHOOL,

on Vine street, above Fourth, erected in 1867, opened 17th of October, 1867.

THE MELROSE SCHOOL,

on Poplar street, above Fourth, erected in 1870, opened 11th of October, 1870.

Both are graded public schools, under the control of the School Directors of the District and under the supervision of the Superintendent of the Common Schools of Northampton County.

The attendance for the school year, ending 1st June, 1872, was—boys 374, girls 341. The average attendance was—boys 282, girls 231. There are 3 male and 3 female teachers employed in Penrose, and 3 male and 4 female teachers in Melrose. The School Board, at this writing, is constituted as follows:

President.—H. Stanley Goodwin.

Secretary.—O. R. Wilt.

Treasurer.—James Purcell.

Directors.—H. K. Shaner, Wm. S. Sieger, Wm. H. Rudolph, Charles Quinn, Hugh O'Neil, Henry McCool and Patrick Downey.

THE NORTHAMPTON CONSERVATIVE,

Milton F. Cushing, proprietor and publisher, was the first weekly newspaper published in the borough of South Bethlehem. The first number was issued 30th of September 1868.

THE MORNING PROGRESS,

O. B. Sigley & Co., proprietors and publishers, was the first daily published in the borough of South Bethlehem. The first number was issued 3d of April, 1871.

THE PRESBYTERIAN CHURCH OF SOUTH BETHLEHEM,

on the corner of Fourth and Vine streets, erected in 1870 and 1871. The lecture room was opened for Divine worship 9th of April, 1871.

First Pastor.—Rev. J. Albert Rondthaler.

First Session.—Rev. J. Albert Rondthaler, W. Calvin Ferriday, W. A. McCormick.

Present Pastor.—Rev. J. Thompson Osler.

The congregation numbers 60 souls; the membership numbers 30.

THE FIRST REFORMED CHURCH OF SOUTH BETHLEHEM,

on Fourth street, between New and Vine, erected in 1870 and 1871, opened for Divine worship 22d of October, 1871.

Pastor.—Rev. N. Z. Snyder.

Number of communicants 125; total membership 226.

THE ANTHRACITE BUILDING,

on Lehigh street, near the old Philadelphia road, erected in 1871, contains the offices of the banking house of E. P. Wilbur & Co., established in October of 1870; the coal offices of Linderman, Skeer & Co., the Franklin Coal Company, and Cleaver & Brodhead; and the offices of "The Morning Progress;" "The Times" Job Print, D. J. Godshalk & Co.; and the Central Express.

THE SOUTH BETHLEHEM READING ROOM AND LIBRARY ASSOCIATION,

in Hartman's Hall, on Fourth street, near New, established in January of 1872. The reading room was formally opened 3d of June, 1872.

President.—Wm. Palfrey.

Vice-President.—B. F. Hittell, M. D.

Secretary.—A. L. Cope.

Corresponding Secretary.—Monroe Van Billiard.

Executive Committee.—George Ziegenfuss, Esq., James McMahon, M. Van Billiard.

THE COLD SPRING WATER COMPANY,

incorporated 8th of April, 1872, by the Court of Lehigh County.

"The object of this corporation is to supply Fountain Hill, Delaware avenue and their vicinity with water for culinary, household and other useful and ornamental purposes."

President.—Abraham Yost.

Secretary and Treasurer.—John L. Cooper.

Directors.—G. B. Linderman, G. H. Daugherty, H. Stanley Goodwin.

THE FOUNTAIN HILL CEMETERY COMPANY,

incorporated 10th of April, 1872, by the Court of Lehigh County, recently located a cemetery for the joint use of the churches of South Bethlehem and its vicinity, on a plot of 6 acres of ground (it was known in mediaeval times as "*Das Buchweizenfeld,*" *i. e.*, The Buckwheat Field), occupying the extreme western limit of the old Hoffert Farm.

The officers of this association are—

President.—George Ziegenfuss.

Vice-President.—H. K. Shaner.

Secretary.—O. K. Wilt. Twelve Directors complete the company's Executive Board.

The first interment within the borders of this cemetery was that of Henry, an infant son of Jacob and Rebecca Bingel, 28th of August, 1872.

www.ingramcontent.com/pod-product-compliance
Lightning Source LLC
LaVergne TN
LVHW021359110826
845150LV00007B/1717

* 9 7 8 1 4 2 5 5 1 3 1 7 7 *